LOST
Virginity

P. L. JONES

Tellwell Talent
www.tellwell.ca

ISBN
978-0-2288-6696-1 (Hardcover)
978-0-2288-6695-4 (Paperback)
978-0-2288-6697-8 (eBook)

Chapter One

AS I SIT HERE ON this plane, I wonder how on earth I got here. I was meant to be at university like most of my friends. Am I really doing the right thing? *Too late now,* I say to myself as the plane takes off.

Here I was just nineteen years old. In fact, my birthday was the day before, so I was literally just nineteen. I had made up my mind NOT to go to university. This decision came about as the result of many things. It was 1969.

I suppose by today's standards, we (my friends and I) were what would be called nerds. We were growing up in what was later referred to as "the swinging 60s" and we swung, but to a different beat—our beat. Drugs, sex and booze were alien to us but NOT rock and roll. No, we liked our music, school dances, house parties and the like. We had fun—real fun—not drunken, stoned or screwing fun. We just didn't see the need for any of it to have fun.

Our stimulus of choice at a party was Coke—not cocaine—Coca-Cola, the pop. Sure, pot was around then (I suppose a lot of it), and it was smoked but not by my friends (mostly). Of course, in the 60s, pot was illegal, and more importantly, criminal. You got busted for having and/or smoking it. I often wonder if that was half the appeal of it, the danger of getting caught if you smoked up. BUSTED, BUSTED, BUSTED. Booze wasn't around for my crowd either. I suppose some drank, but I never saw them do it. I would never let anyone smoke pot in front of me. I didn't care who they were. If they insisted, I would leave or throw them out if it were in my house.

We didn't use the really coarse swear words—no particular reason why not. They just seemed a bit stupid to me. We had snappy sayings instead—groovy (you must know that one), fab, snap, a gas, blast, bummer, far out, neato, goody snap (I made that one up myself—don't know why, just liked the sound of it.)

Hippies had their own sayings—some good, some just plain stupid. They had a point sometimes, but just went about it in a weird way. As far as I was concerned, they were dropouts who thought everyone owed them a living. I site a few examples of this later on in this book when I had real live contact with these guys.

From what I could make out, all this free love they preached translated into a lot of sex and drugs. This meant a lot of stoned guys spreading a lot of STDs and unwanted, unplanned babies. Ever been to a commune? If so, you know what I'm talking about. If not, you missed nothing, believe me.

I do realize I'm painting a picture of a bunch of goody two-shoes geeks here, but I assure you that we were nothing of the kind. Neither were we ugly, stupid, lazy, miserable, mean, or any other negative adjective to describe a geek you can think of. We did well in school, had boyfriends/girlfriends, worked hard, had a great social life with each other and other people, had jobs, joined clubs and some (like me) volunteered our time to help others. We were the nice teenagers of the 60s.

A lot, and I mean a lot, of my friends were guys. No sexual undertones at all, we were just friends (as far as I was concerned). Their dicks may have had different ideas unknown to me. I lived in my own world (that didn't include sex), so I wouldn't have realized anything else. Nor did I care.

To this end, I now include a snap of myself. I would be around sixteen years old in this photo. The lady on the left is my mother.

A party to us was a place to dance, make out, talk and laugh but mostly dance. School dances were usually on a Friday night, and we all went—to dance and try to find a boyfriend. You can tell a lot about a guy by the way he dances (or tries to). The fact that he bothered to make an effort was sometimes enough. There's nothing more intimate than slow, slow, ever so slow dancing with someone you like or even love. How romantic!

We also had a lot of house parties. Many of them ended up at my house for some reason. I guess we had a big house and a nice rec room. House parties were great because you could find sneaky places to make out with someone—maybe your boyfriend at the time. When I say make out, that's what I mean. We didn't have sex (penetration). We called that "going all the way." Some did, I guess, but I'm pretty sure not at my house—there were too many people around. Some who did got pregnant, which was a big deal back then.

My own brother knocked up his girlfriend when they both were in high school. She had the baby and gave it up for adoption. They later married and then divorced because he didn't keep his pecker in his pants.

Back then, we didn't know a lot about sex. We had health class, but that was teaching information about our physical bodies—nothing on what sex was, how to do it, or contraception etc. No wonder those who chose sex mostly got pregnant. There's a good quote from a movie called *Definitely Maybe*. It's said by Abigail Breslin, who plays Ryan Reynold's young daughter. After she learns about sex at school, she says, "If they didn't want babies, how come they had sex?" Says it all for me.

There is an old song whose lyrics go like this: "If you can't be with the one you love, love the one you're with." What a stupid philosophy to have. Most of the 60s proved that. Shouldn't sex be special or at least with someone you know? Nowadays, they call it casual sex. How can the most intimate thing two people can do be casual?

Now that you can see the environment I grew up in, I'll go into more detail about my personal life. I wanted to be a teacher while I was in high school. More to the point, I wanted to be a high school teacher. Even more to the point, I wanted to be a high school French teacher. This was inspired by my Grade 10 French teacher. At that time, French was not taught in grade school or even part of high school, mostly it was an option (like Latin, which I also took). I loved French and my Grade 10 French teacher. What a guy he was, and he really inspired us to learn the language. Years later, it turned out he was gay. We didn't even suspect. His partner was my Grade 13 English teacher. It wasn't a shock, we just didn't know anything about the queer culture. Nobody came out of any closets in the 60s.

Since I studied French in the 60s, we were told that we were learning "proper" French. Quebec French was considered to be inferior then. There was a comparison made between these two styles of French alongside a similar comparison between Cockney English and the Queen's English. They are both English, but one is easier to understand than the other. I had personal experience with this when I was a teenager. While studying French in high school, I had this good friend called Jean-Louis who was studying to be an electrician. We made this deal that I would help him with his math and he would help me with my French. Well, it didn't work out because he was from Gaspé, and I couldn't understand his French. Since he spoke little English, that killed the math help on my part. I don't know if this difference between Quebecois French and European French still exists or not.

In my teens, I grew up in Toronto—Bayview and Sheppard to be precise. I have four brothers, only one of which I can even stand or get along with. Both my parents were a mess, and as such, the five of us didn't really turn out all that well. How could we have, being raised by a jerk and a drunk? The latter (my mother) was a result of the former (my father). The examples of garbage that happened because of them could fill a whole book by itself. I'll only go into some that effected me.

In Grade 10, I found out I needed braces on my teeth. My bite was all wrong. My top jaw was too forward, so my teeth didn't meet properly. Over time, my teeth would grind themselves down. The orthodontist agreed that my dad could make payments. I guess even then it was very expensive.

Every tooth needed to be done. By the word "done," I mean have a metal ring (no idea what kind) hammered around each tooth. I can remember him saying to me, "Just cup your two hands and put them under your jaw." I suppose that was so my bottom jaw didn't snap off. PAIN? Fifty some odd years later, I can still feel the pain. But the top teeth were the worst as there wasn't anyway to hold the top of my head. It literally felt as if my head would come off. Once all the teeth were ringed, and the metal wire stretched and put in place, he tightened the wire at the back of the four teeth. I had hooks on which I placed elastics (fun while eating). This was to force the jaw back as well. At night, I had to wear a harness which was inserted into my back teeth at the top and went around my neck. This was also tightened at every visit. You also have to remember that they were very attractive when I smiled which wasn't very often as you can image. I had puffed out teeth and lips. I take you back to my photo a few pages back. See how full and puffy my lips are? All braces. My real lips are so thin and horrible that I still won't and never have worn lipstick. Does this sound painful and embarrassing? Well, it was. But I was assured it would only be for a year—my Grade 10 year.

Guess who had a fight with the doctor and wouldn't make the payments? Yep. My father. So, the orthodontist refused to work at all on my teeth. I had braces on my teeth for all four years of high school until my mom and I paid off the bill, and they were finally taken off. I just had to wear a retainer for awhile.

In Grade 9, I took typing. An easy course and easy good mark, or so I thought. Who knew repeating fff and jjj a million times would teach you to type? But I surely learned how to type. This single course did more for me in getting jobs than anything else in my life. I think nowadays, babies are born knowing how to type, only it's called "texting" now. By the time they're in Grade 9, they would make me look incompetent. Still, with all that plodding, repetitive lessons, you did learn to type.

So much so that in the summer between Grades 9 and 10, I worked for my dad doing typing. He owned a collection agency. My job was to type names and addresses on threatening letters to deadbeats who didn't pay their bills. I was paid $25 a week. Out of that, I had to pay for my bus fares, clothing, food etc. I had to take the bus and subway to downtown Toronto, as my dad was never home long enough to drive me.

His office was in the Flatiron building where Front and Wellington Streets meet in Toronto. I loved it. There was this really old elevator with a steel mesh door (like you see in movies about Paris). I thought I was the cat's ass as I was only fourteen years old (fifteen in September) and was making money and having a ball. I felt so grown-up, and I guess, for my age, I really was.

This was the summer of 1964. If you have seen or know the Flatiron building, it has steel fire escapes down the left-hand side of it. I used to eat my lunch out there (even though I'm deathly afraid of heights). One afternoon, I could hear screaming, loud noises, and shouting coming from the north. I asked the women I worked with what the noise was all about. They told me the Beatles were staying at the King Eddy. The King Edward Hotel was on King Street just up from Wellington. As I didn't know who the Beatles were at the time, this didn't impress me. I didn't even walk up to check it out. How stupid was that! I have lived to regret that day, but there you go. Live and learn, eh? I was never a groupy or a group follower per se. I liked their music, but that was all.

It was during this summer that I found out what a disgusting pig my father was. The first time I knew anything was wrong was when my father yelled at me for telling my mother that he was screwing around on her. I didn't need to act innocent because I was. I had no idea he was doing this—all I got was, "Then how did your mom know?"

"How the hell do I know!?" I shouted.

When he faced my mom, she confessed that one of the salesmen told her, and she blamed me because she didn't want him to be fired. So, I took the blame instead. My father had set this woman up in business and even had the nerve to have me work for her (well, before I knew who she was).

I guessed this wasn't the first infidelity, but it sent my mom over the edge. She ended up having a nervous breakdown, which was treated with pills on the doctor's part, and alcohol on her part. She was always drunk. I had two brothers under the age of ten, so it wasn't a good situation. My old man didn't care. He got a suite at Sutton Place, which was an exclusive residence back then. Cadillac was the car of his choice. We had two parked in our driveway most of the time. We had no money to buy gas, but it looked good. Years later, I found out that all my friends had thought we were rich.

I was stuck in the middle of something no teenager should be involved in, but I had to look after my mom. There was a job opening at Bayview Village (the local mall) in the bakery. I made her get all dressed up to apply for it. I watched as she walked the four corners of the intersection and sat until some time had passed. Then she came home and said she didn't get the job. So, I took her hand and walked her to the bakery. She got the job. The only thing I credit myself with was that I made her go. She got that job all by herself.

All during my teenage years, my mom was a mess. My dad would come home sometimes, mostly for sex, and she let him. Once, I found the negatives from his polaroid camera in MY closet. They were dirty pictures he'd taken of her. Something to show his buddies, I guess.

Although she had her job, she still drank. Wouldn't you? Luckily, she did have to go to work, so that helped a lot.

There was one night—I don't know where she had been, but she came home in a taxi as drunk as anyone could be. I had a girlfriend over that night, and when we went into my room, we could see a man standing there. My mom was lying on the bed, half naked with only the important bits exposed for his use. He had undone his pants and was getting out his dick to rape my mother when I jumped on his back and started smacking him in the head. Boy, did he move—down the stairs—out the door—in his taxi and gone. Guess nobody told him anyone was home. My girlfriend just stood there with her eyes wide open, crying. We got my mom to bed so she could sleep it off.

Speaking of attempted rape, I had a few bouts of that myself. The one that stands out the most for me was near my house. I had been at my friends, and coming home, I cut through the People's Church parking lot. It was very dark, but I never thought anything of it and had done it a million times before. In that parking lot were a group of guys—no idea how old they were. They spotted me and came after me. There was no question what was on their minds. Just before they reached me, car lights came from nowhere, and I ran just as they were being blinded. Home was only a few blocks away, and I ran all the way. When I got home, there was nobody there to help me, so I called my friend and her mother told me to call the police. When they came, I regretted even calling them. They made me feel like it was all my fault and certainly weren't going to look for the guys or help me in any way. It didn't help that the house looked like pigs lived in it.

Before and after that happened to me, I've had numerous boys/men make passes, try to rape, touch, feel up—any expression you want to use for abuse. We didn't have "me too" then—you just put up with this stuff or removed yourself from it if you could. I know I lost a really good babysitting job because the lady's husband had friendly hands. I'm quite sure she knew why I left—women aren't quite as stupid as men seem to think.

Later on in life, I went to EMDR therapy to see if either my father or grandfather had abused me in any way. Nothing turned up. Maybe he didn't sexually abuse me, but my father did some stuff that was not to be proud of. He used to regularly grab my foot and bend it completely over to make me say "UNCLE" but I never would. He could have snapped my foot off before I would bend to him like my mom did. He used to ask me if he could show me how a boyfriend would kiss me. Guess my answer. I'd had enough of the male species doing inappropriate stuff to me; I wasn't about to let my dad.

So, this was my world growing up as a teenager in the 60s. Don't get me wrong. I loved school and did very well, had plenty of friends, travelled, worked and saved my money.

To this end, I had money to go on a few trips. My first major trip was to New York City with a girlfriend of mine. We flew there and stayed in a hotel somewhere downtown—can't really remember where. It was probably a real dump, but I remember it as grand. You must remember, we were only sixteen years old. We saw the sights and thought we were terribly grown-up. That's when I got the travel bug. One thing that stood out in my mind during this trip was people in NYC didn't know where Toronto was. Imagine that.

My next trip was in Grade 13 with a different girlfriend to Quebec City. This, of course, was to learn more French not to hook a few cute French guys. Even though their French and the language we learned were different, we got along well. What a beautiful little city. You didn't get the French attitude then that you can get now. They were actually nice to us. Especially a couple of French guys we met and invited back to our room. Friendship went a little too far that day, but we survived. Luckily, we understood what they said, and they didn't know that fact.

So, with these two trips under my belt, I really wanted more, but I was meant to go to university. After all, I had taken Latin so I could. As I have told you, I wanted to be a high school French teacher. This meant I was to go to York University, instead of U of T, where most of my friends would go and their parents could afford to send them there. They didn't come out of university with a loan the size of a house mortgage. Granted, they lived at home, but so what? They didn't have the chance to party their parent's money away.

Chapter Two

SO, ON I PLODDED. I did pretty well in high school. At that time, you could take a four-year or five-year course, depending on what job you wanted. If you were going to university, you needed a five-year course. Primary school was different as well—some went from Grade 1–8. Others only went to Grade 6, and then you went to junior high 7–9. Then high school was 10–13 or 10–12, depending on what you took. To pass Grade 13, you needed seven credits. I took English (two credits), French (two credits), math (two credits), and biology (one credit). I took biology because one of my friends was going to be a nurse and talked me into it. What a mistake that was. I hated it, was bad at it, and more importantly, it brought my average way down. (Good thing I didn't want to be a nurse).

So, I had the grades to go to York University, but I did have to wonder if my father would pay for it. Remember the braces? But before I had a chance to fret over it, something happened that completely, and I mean completely, changed my whole life.

So, in Grade 13, we were to apply for a "career day" in our chosen field. Unfortunately for me, observing high school activities wasn't on the menu, so I had to attend an elementary school. I believe it was a Grade 1 class I observed. What a joke. Apparently, this was the beginning of the notion that kids would learn on their own when they wanted to. So, I got quite an eyeful of something that completely went against everything I stood and still do stand for—logic, organization, order, everything in its place, and discipline. I was, after all, a VIRGO. What I saw was completely wrong. There was a teacher sitting in a corner reading a book to no one (maybe one or two little girls sat in front of her, but that was it). There were no rows of desks—no rows of anything. Most of the boys were bouncing of the walls, playing with toys, or running around. Ask a five- or six-year-old boy if he would rather sit at a desk and look at books or play with a toy—what do you think his answer would be?

I only stayed a short time—I couldn't stand to see what I was looking at. I thought to myself, *how can I become a teacher if this is what it's like?* Of course, it never occurred to me that teaching high school was a completely different thing. That was how big of an impact that short time had on me.

Well, now what to do? I didn't really want to waste a ton of money getting a degree that probably wouldn't get me a job in the end. I loved to travel, so maybe I could do that. I had done some, and I really had fun. Not that New York City and Quebec City were that far away, but I learned that I liked seeing new things and places. Maybe I could take the year off and travel, and then continue with university when I had a clearer idea of what I could get a job doing. Nowadays, they call it a gap year—mostly by rich kids whose parents finance the travel for them. I didn't have rich parents, but I did have my own money from working.

So, a plan started working in my little pee brain. Where? With whom? For how long? I had long since become single, so I had no boyfriend to worry about. My family certainly wouldn't miss me. I had no university to look forward to. I made up my mind that this was the thing to do for myself, and it all sounded quite exciting.

My biggest problem was I needed someone to travel with—a male would be handy in case of trouble. I had a couple of good male friends who were willing to come with me. Then we ran into a problem when they failed a couple of subjects and had to repeat them to pass and graduate. Shit out of luck again.

So, then I had a look at my girl friends. Quite a few were going to nursing and teacher's colleges as well as others to uni. The friend I went to NYC with had just gotten engaged to this creep and was very proud of her ring, so she was out. I call him a creep for a very good reason. A year before this, she had talked me into a double date with some friend of theirs. We went to a drive-in. Of course, the guy thought that this was an open invitation to grope and manhandle me. So, when I didn't play ball, my friend's so-called fiancé knocked HER around. When I asked what happened, she wouldn't admit it, but that's what happened. I would've given anything if she would come travel with me as I knew her fiancé wouldn't have waited for her. I guess she knew it too and didn't want to take the chance.

So now what was I to do??? I guessed I could just go to university to get some degree, but then what?

Luckily for me, the word got around that I needed someone to travel with, and a girl I didn't really know said she'd like to join me. We were going. More importantly, I was going!

I was working that summer, and Grade 13 had ended in June, so we both had time to earn the needed money to do this travelling. We decided on September as a departure date.

There was a great deal to do in a short time. Passports were sent for, money was saved. When it came to buying our tickets, we needed advice. You have to remember we were both eighteen years old. We went to Brotherton's Travel Agency and Yonge St. near Sheppard Ave. We decided on Europe, and we were told the cheapest way to get to there was to fly from NYC to Luxembourg. We would have a stopover in Reykjavik, Iceland for one night. These were open ended tickets and were good for a year. So, we had a year to bugger about and see what we could get up to. But it also meant that if things went wrong, we (or I) could come back home after making the way back to Luxembourg. This is the same flight the travel writer Bill Bryson refers to in his book, *Neither Here Nor There*, only he did it in 1972, not 1969. He does not say he stopped overnight in Reykjavik just refuelled there.

Back then, there were no computers to fire up and get information about countries etc., no reviews, and no planned itineraries for you to copy. You did your own research and planned yourself. Except, we decided to wing it and just go wherever whenever. We booked two seats for Friday September 19th to Luxembourg. That was when the seat price dropped even further. As I've said, it was one day after I turned nineteen.

So, the summer passed – working, babysitting, packing, getting everything ready for the off as they say. I would miss my graduation as it was held in the end of September for those graduating from Grade 13. That was OK by me. I don't like that kind of stuff. I knew I did well and that was enough for me.

I got traveller's cheques totaling $650. It sounded like a lot of money since I had worked so hard and so long to earn it but of course I knew nothing of what lodging, food, travel by bus, train or boat would cost. Of course, in 1969, there were NO bank cards and NO credit cards, just money (cash) and personal cheques. I was quite sure nobody in Europe would take a Canadian personal cheque. So, cash it was in the form of traveller's cheques.

I had to get a sort of sheet/sleeping bag for the youth hostels, and of course, join the organization. I bought a small black suitcase. I knew I'd have to lug it around by myself (no such thing as wheels on cases then), so I couldn't take a lot of stuff.

We decided to take the bus to New York from downtown Toronto—the same one that is still there now in 2020, and unfortunately, pretty well in the same condition as it was fifty years ago. We were booked for a night flight from JFK, so we had to take an early morning bus to NYC to get to the airport in time.

I spent the night at my mom's apartment. She and my dad were getting a divorce, so our fancy Bayview house had to be sold. Didn't she just scrub it from top to bottom to sell it. She moved with four sons (two of which were quite young, ten and eleven) to an apartment off Sheppard Avenue in Willowdale. Well, only one of the brothers even bothered to get out of bed to say goodbye to me (my mom was at work).

When I got to the bus station, all of my friend's family were there with her to say goodbye. Typical of my life—on my own again. We had an uneventful bus ride to New York—how much trouble can you get into while sitting on a bus? Although, I did get quite a shock when Lynn lit up a cigarette. I didn't know she smoked. I don't remember any feelings of excitement or much of anything else for that matter. It never occurred to us that we were just two teenage girls going to who knew where, to do who knew what. I don't know about Lynn, but I thought it was great. I actually really thought I was doing the best thing I could do for my circumstances—no boyfriend, no university, no family to speak of. But I had some money, the travel bug, and someone to travel with. No turning back now.

Chapter Three

OUR FLIGHT TO REYKJAVIK FROM JFK was one and a half hours with a delay by Icelandic Airline. Once on board, I remember they served some sort of fish—not my favourite food. In fact, I only eat heavily battered halibut from the fish and chip shop. Either during the flight, or maybe it began on the bus, I started to feel sick. I tried to sleep, but that's not always easy on a plane. Maybe all of it was starting to catch up to me and that was my reaction. Who knows?

I had written a diary during some of this trip, so I will refer to it starting now. I have a pretty good memory, but some fifty plus years have gone by, and I might not remember all that happened correctly.

It was cold (38°F) upon landing in Iceland and very barren looking. The hotel was very nice and quite fancy. We were given a lovely room with its own bathroom (not a given then in these places). There was good food "mais je suis trop malade de manger." Quotes are taken from my diary. The plane was delayed again flying to Luxembourg. We had already lost four hours flying to Iceland and now another hour to Luxembourg. We arrived at about 2:00 a.m. and took a bus to the city centre where we sat up all night in a café because we were too cheap to pay for a hotel just for a few hours.

The next day, we walked and walked and walked, seeing the town. It was clean, very old, and it had this new red bridge running through it which spoilt the old-world effect. I was really disappointed not to see any castles as I had supposed they always were around in Europe. We met two German guys who helped us and showed us around. They were very nice to us and spoke a little English. The people here spoke both German and French very well, so we were not bad with the French ones.

The Youth Hostel didn't impress. It was my first and last one I stayed in. The sleeping bag thing I brought certainly did come in handy though. The room was clean and had ten bunks in one room. The girls were mostly American with very few Canadians and others thrown in for good luck. Four of the American girls had just travelled from Italy. The country didn't impress them at all.

"You had to put salt and pepper on the spaghetti to make it edible because it was so bland," one complained. "And the guys kept groping us and yelling stuff at us."

Well, I kept my mouth shut. I knew a lot of Italians in Toronto. Spaghetti sauce for Italians is just about smashed up tomatoes and not much else. The guys do grab you and say stupid things. It wouldn't have bothered me, as I was used to it. Anyway, I kind of made up my mind that maybe Italy wouldn't be one of our next stops. I didn't leave Toronto for more of the same.

We left the hostel around 9 a.m. It was a warm, sunny, bright day to explore. We walked to a nearby restaurant to have breakfast. That was a very expensive breakfast as I thought I'd be clever and steal some butter for later use. I was so clever that I put it in my bag along with my camera. Of course, the butter ruined it. So now I had ruined butter, a ruined camera, and no more photos until I replaced the camera.

We met this guy, Bob, who was hitchhiking as well, and we thought it might be a good idea to have a male travelling partner with us as a few girls had just been raped while hitchhiking just about where we were. Bob was an American draft dodger over to buy a bike from Germany. I guess he thought travelling with us was a good idea too, and maybe we made him look a little more human. (He was very scruffy looking and looked like how a biker was supposed to look, I guess.)

We hitchhiked with him to Echternach in Luxembourg. Pretty little place with a nice school and some memorable fountains. We then got a ride to the German border where we were picked up by a guy in a truck who took us to a little village in Belgium called Herve. I remember looking at the speedometer and thinking how fast we were going, but of course, we were in kilometers, not miles, so to me we were going fast.

Well, the driver of the truck had very friendly hands. We all had to crowd into the cab of the truck, and I was beside the driver with my legs on either side of the gear shift. Every time he shifted gears, he got a nice feel of my crotch. There was nothing I could do except give him dirty looks which really stopped him. I wish. I don't remember how long the drive was, but it was, and still remains to this day, one of the worse drives of my life. Thank God we had Bob with us, or who knows what would've happened to Lynn and I.

Anyway, we got to Herve quite late and met a bunch of French guys who took us to a place where we could sleep for the night. They were a very nice family called the Hendricks who had eleven children and were kind enough to take us in. Even with all those kids, they had a nice room for Lynn and I. I don't remember where Bob slept. I didn't care really because I had a bed in a family house. Imagine a family with eleven kids taking in three strangers, feeding them, putting them up, and making them feel like a part of their family. And what food they fed us (of course, home-cooked), great big plates of food like Europeans eat. We tried to pay them back by raking grass and helping to clean up.

I remember the friendliness of everyone. Shaking hands and kissing when they said hello and goodbye, it was so removed from the cold and unfeeling place we had come from. I was beginning to appreciate the place we were in and loving Europe and its way of life. It was so laid-back compared to my old world.

But, after a couple of nights, it was time to say goodbye to everyone and not impose on them anymore. We left the Hendricks around 9 a.m. and picked up a few rides on our way to Rotterdam, Netherlands.

We ended up spending a few nights in this horrible, tiny, freezing cold cabin. God only knows exactly where we were. Lynn and I had bunk beds, and Bob slept on the floor. It was so very cold. True to myself, I caught a stinking cold to top it off. I remember outside reminded me a bit of the 401 in Toronto. It was some sort of highway and looked very cold and barren looking. Lynn had enough nerve to have a shower in freezing cold water. I begged out as my cold was getting worse. That was the first shower since Iceland for Lynn. I still had to wait for mine. JOY!!! My very long hair looked awful, and I'm sure I smelled real bad. I didn't really care. Travelling like this, you quickly learn what's really important to survive. Bob was a good friend and protector to us.

The first thing that hit me about Rotterdam (besides the rain and cold) were the bikes. Bikes were everywhere—kids on bikes, people on motorbikes. They had a special lane just for them. Old hat here now, but that wasn't always the case in North America. Don't forget, this was 1969, and bikes in North America were not tolerated very well.

We had walks around Rotterdam, but it's hard to enjoy a place when you're so very cold and also have a cold. I remember washrooms (public) being awful and having no toilet paper. So, you got in the habit of taking napkins at meal time to wipe your ass later. We went to a modern ballet to try to keep warm. I LOVE ballet and studied it as a child. I didn't like the modern stuff very much then nor now. Don't jazz up ballet—leave it be.

We took the bus to the Hague, Netherlands. I didn't really take much notice of it. "Politique ville," I wrote in my diary. We had no desire to stay there even overnight. The only good thing was that the weather was warming up and getting sunny. This was the end of September, after all.

What a cool place Amsterdam is. It wasn't a cool place for me back then for the same reason it was and is for a lot of people now. Namely, the drugs, sex and prostitution were mostly all legal, and are still legal to this day. I didn't know any of that when I visited the place in 1969.

We thumbed our way from the Hague to Amsterdam in two rides. We stayed the first night in a student hotel, not to be confused with a student hostel which has less rules and regs. I FINALLY washed my hair in COLD water. The hotel was clean, but had no hot water. What's this with the no hot water deal? Can't these people heat water? Maybe they just didn't want us to have any. I must've smelled great. I guess we all did, so nobody noticed me in particular.

We got up early. Breakfast was included in the price of the room. They had cheese, bread, salami, cold cuts, boiled eggs, tea and coffee. It was a strange breakfast for me, but it was food, and it was free. And it was good food. I especially remember that the bread was excellent.

So off we walked to see some of the city. The streets were so narrow with all the canals cutting through all over the place. The city was one of the prettiest I had ever seen. To me, it was so European. They did drive like crazy, and I often wondered how long it would be before someone hit me. We went to a big museum (no idea its name) to see an art exhibition by Rembrandt. We also went to his house.

To get from guilders to Canadian dollars, you divided by about three and a half. You soon got used to doing it quickly so you didn't get ripped off. My math lessons certainly came in handy as I needed to do everything in my head—no calculators for our use.

We moved to another place with a canal right under our window. Lynn and I had a room with two beds, and Bob slept outside the room, but he actually got a bed this time. This place had HOT HOT water with showers for 8 guilders without breakfast (about $2). When I say they had hot water, well it was only warm, but it felt very hot to me. When you travel like this, you quickly learn what's really important to survive—food, sleep, a washroom, a shower and warm water. Finally, we had it all. Of course, as with everywhere we had been, you shared the bathroom with the whole world. That was OK because we had access to one, and that's all we cared about. We bought bread, chocolate milk, butter and cookies for supper. After all, we were in Amsterdam.

They spoke a lot more English in Amsterdam than Rotterdam, and the weather was a lot warmer. Thank God. Stairs are very narrow there, so you sort of walked up and down sideways. We were four flights up of course. They have ropes from windows so they can haul stuff up or down from floor to floor without using the stairs.

I bought my mom some wooden shoes with slippers in them and sent them off. Can't imagine she'd even care or wear them, but it made me feel better. They cost me 18.50 guilders (about $4). I had written letters and post cards to my friends and family with no replies. We could get mail from the American Express Offices that were scattered all over the place in Europe. I didn't really take into account that it probably took a week or more for my letters to get to Canada and the same for their reply. So really, I probably had tons of mail in offices of past travel.

We visited Anne Frank's house, and it was very frightening to me. You read about these things, but to see it in person packed a punch. I just liked walking around the city, looking at the canals, parks, sights etc. It was the nicest place we had seen so far.

I cashed my first traveller's cheque, so I guess I was doing quite well with money. I always have been good with money, and it comes in handy when you're on your own in a foreign country. I didn't count on Lynn, who could leave anytime she wanted. You soon learn to be self-reliant as a necessity.

Bob stayed in bed all day because he had caught my cold. I often wondered about Bob and Lynn and whether or not they were sleeping together. I still don't know—it was none of my business who she slept with. With Bob in bed all day, Lynn and I went shopping. It was just something for us to do without a man under foot. He wasn't interested anyway. We just window shopped as we had no money for anything else. We would also have to carry anything we bought.

We ended up in the red light district. Of course, we had no idea it was there, but we soon clued in. The hookers were half-dressed in well-lit rooms facing the street, waiting for their services to be used by someone. You saw signs for live sex acts, sex stores, life-sized billboards of naked people doing things to each other. We were glad Bob wasn't with us. He'd probably already been here by himself and maybe he was into this stuff. Who knew? I didn't even know how old he was. Old enough to be draft dodger, that's for sure.

The next morning, we got up early. Lynn and Bob had fought the night before (hence my guess that they were sleeping together). Anyway, we walked down to the Heineken brewery where we had a walking tour of the place and afterward could drink as much beer as you wanted. I only tried a glass—beer makes me fart and pee a lot. Bob and Lynn got stuck into the beer though. Pretty good for 10 a.m.

I decided to give them some space to fix their problem and went on a long, long walk by myself along the pretty canals, skinny houses, lovely architecture and gardens. It was nice to not talk to anyone or ask where they might want to go next. I went to Dam Square (the main place for gathering in Amsterdam, similar to Piccadilly Circus in London, England), down Damrak Street, and up a tiny colourful side street just down from where we were staying. I enjoyed the warmer weather without any rain. I headed back home to shower and wash my hair.

The next morning, we saw Bob off. He was heading to Munich to pick up his bike. Maybe he wanted Lynn to go with him, and she really didn't want to. I will never know exactly what happened with those two. Although I was travelling with her, I didn't really know her well enough to pry into her personal life. But I must say, it was comforting to have Bob along during our hitchhiking days. God only knows what would've happened to us. Now what would we do? No more Bob.

The city of Amsterdam had some sort of protest demonstration on Damrak with speeches etc. Very peaceful. Lynn wanted to join in, but it wasn't anything to do with us, so we left. It was so warm and sunny that day that we didn't even need to wear a coat. Good thing. My light beige three-quarter jacket was filthy. I had slept in it, travelled in it, and done just about everything in it. It was only October 5th—just over two weeks after leaving home.

We sat for hours watching some guy's jacket on Dam Square. It was a lovely place to watch people. Offers of hash and pot floated by all the time. Lynn had her fair share. I don't know if she paid for it, nor did I care.

"You don't really know what you're smoking, do you?" I protested to deaf ears.

I wasn't interested. The fact was that you didn't know what was in the joint. Having a bit of wine now and then was enough for me.

I had cashed three $30 traveller's cheques in Amsterdam. Even back then, it was an expensive place. Of course, we were paying for rooms, meals, entertainment etc., so the money soon went.

When we got home, three—count them three—men had moved into where Bob had lived. That meant that every time we went into our room, we had to climb through them and their stuff.

I think we decided to leave Amsterdam that day. London was our next destination.

I remember some American girl saying to us, "If you ever get to London, that will be the end of travelling because you'll stay there."

Chapter Four

WE BOUGHT OUR FERRY TICKETS to London. It cost 58 guilders—a fortune to us as we had mostly been hitchhiking which was free (apart from the odd grope). But without Bob, we knew our hitchhiking days were over.

I had always wanted to see England. My grandmother on my mother's side was from Bolton in Lancashire. She always wanted to go back but never did. So, I was going for her.

We left Amsterdam early and took the train to Haarlem and then on to Hoek van Holland. The ferry ride to Harwich, England was really bumpy but quite enjoyable.

My diary reads "bloody English money." This was just before the conversion to metric and certainly not easy to understand. Apparently, their money was divided into pounds, shillings and pennies. So, eight pounds, four shillings, and fourpence would be written £8/4/4d. There were twenty shillings in a pound. There were many off shoots of this, but this will do for now. I never did learn the rest. The country did not officially switch to decimal until February 15th 1971, so I had to deal with the way it was and not just pounds and pence like now.

We met this hash-head called Mac who lived in London. He took us on the London Underground which is called the tube by Londoners. We ended up at an English girl's house. I slept on the couch, and Mac and Lynn had the floor. Imagine again a stranger taking in two girls overnight just because we were there. All Mac did was smoke hash like it was giving him life. I supposed Lynn joined in. I didn't care. I was too tired and went to sleep.

I slept late and woke with a backache. I was beat. I took the tube to an American Express office, but as usual, no letters from anyone. We tried to find a flat, which wasn't easy because we couldn't get the phones to work. Everything was backwards here—driving, walking, crossing the road, the money, and now the phones.

We finally gave up and booked a hotel. You really do get sick of sleeping on floors or couchs after a while. It was £3 a night for a double room which was a fortune considering a week's rental of a bedsit was only £4. But we had a bath and washed our hair. We both had long straight hair, so not washing it was a big deal to us. You must be clean to walk the streets of London.

The next day, we learned how to use the phones. You didn't put the money in until someone answered the phone! I suspect this has a lot to do with the English (they are cheap) not forking out money until they are sure they have the right person. People generally answered their phone with their phone number, not "Hi."

We finally found a flat in southwest London—the area of Fulham to be precise. The house was called Fortescue House and was on Waldemar Ave. The nearest tube station was Parsons Green. I was waiting outside the house for Lynn to get our keys when a real scruffy guy asked if he could let me in.

"Can I let you in, luv?" he asked.

"No, thanks," I said coldly and not very friendly.

You never know who these guys are, do you? Thank God Lynn came then with the keys. We were on the top floor, and our room had bunk beds, would you believe? It was like we were back in the youth hostel again. I told Lynn she'd have to have the top, and she didn't mind. We had a stove—or so we thought. Of course, the stupid thing didn't work. The bathroom (the loo to the English) was right next door, so we got to hear some lovely sounds all night long. This meant six guys and two girls were all sharing one tiny little bathroom. The same bathroom that was right beside our bedroom.

Turns out the creep who wanted to let me in was our next-door neighbour. His name was John, and he was staying with another guy named Pete. They were both from Hull (in Yorkshire). Well, didn't they think they hit the jackpot! Two birds to do all the cooking for them on our stove. We soon straightened them out. Besides the two next door, there was this very intense Greek guy, Tacus, who played nonstop with his worry beads. He was a studying to be an engineer. Then there was this gorgeous, posh bloke called Andy. I liked Andy. He was also a student—don't know what of. He had a girlfriend of course, but we got along as friends. Then we had two Aussies sharing a double room downstairs. I never thought much of either of them. Dennis and John were their names. John (my next-door neighbour) had a girlfriend he saw once a week for a quick shag in her Mini. The rest of the time, he was free to do whatever he wanted. I later learned this was mostly how English guys treated their girlfriends/wives. Pete was on his own but a real disaster in his own right. He could knock anything and everything over just by getting up. Then he got embarrassed and farted, all with a bright red face. You had to feel sorry for him—he tried so hard to please. Unfortunately, he liked me, so I tried to be as nice as I could to him. We would/could never be more than friends. I'd have to control my laughter. But he was nice enough and always good to me.

This was October 9th and London was warm and sunny. It was not what I expected. Back then, London was noted for its smog. They had cans of it around Piccadilly for the tourists to buy. I guess you let out the smog when you open the can. Anyway, all the Londoners seemed to think this weather was marvelous. It was just a normal fall to us. You soon learn that if it's not raining in London, it's a fine day even when overcast or foggy.

So, we settled into life in London for the time being—not really knowing if our travels would end here like predicted in Amsterdam. It was nice to be in one place even if just for a while.

One of the guys next door and Andy took me to a pub—my first. Someone was playing the piano and singing. I could really see the attraction for these places. It was nice there. But, I didn't really drink, so I had to watch myself as it would've taken very little to get me drunk. I didn't really know these six guys, and yet I was living with them in the same building without locks on the doors. Plenty of men had already tried their luck with me when I was sober. So, I had two baby shams—cheap champagne I think it was supposed to be. It was sweet enough that I could drink it and it didn't appear to be very alcoholic. We went back to my room and talked until late.

The next day (with no hangover at all—you never know), I slept in and went to the laundromat. Andy came up and we talked all the afternoon. He was a nice guy. We had fish and chips for dinner. Of course we did—we were in England.

That night, me, Lynn, John and Pete went to a different pub. One of the guys put a pint of beer in front of me.

"What am I supposed to do with that?" I laughed.

"Drink it," came the answer.

I tried but only got about halfway down the glass. A pint is a lot of beer. We came home again and stayed up late, drinking tea and talking. They had a radio and a record player next door, so that was a treat for us.

The next day, Lynn and I went to the nearest American Express, but there were still no letters for me. I was giving up hope of ever getting news from home. We had ravioli for dinner and met a waiter who invited us to Hyde Park on Sunday. They have what is called Speakers' Corner on Sundays where mostly crazy people stand up on whatever they can and shout, scream, and talk about whatever they want. Very interesting to watch, but no way would I ever participate.

Since it appeared we had settled into London to live for awhile, I went to PD Bureau on Shaftesbury Ave. and got a job. I got the name and address of this place in Toronto just in case. PD Bureau was an employment agency offering temporary jobs to local and foreign workers. This was Friday, and I started work on Monday. I made 10/6 per hour (about $1) which was a lot more than I had ever earned before. Thank God I took Grade 9 typing and worked for my father all those years.

Work in London in 1969 was plentiful—obviously, when a foreigner could get a job the same day. I still had lots of money left, but I figured even if the job was short term, I'd earn some of the money I'd already spent so far. At that time, you didn't need a work permit or visa to work in the UK. You could stay a year in Britain without any papers with a review in six months. That open-ended ticket really came in handy, as I knew I had a way home if they threw me out of the country.

Lynn wasn't interested in working quite yet. She said she had plenty of money left and wanted to have some fun. We toured around London, walking and seeing sights. It was lovely, and I fell in love with the city. It remains to this day my favourite place to live and visit. It is so old, cultured, and interesting, with so much to keep anyone busy for ages.

A major drawback was the food. I remember eating a sandwich once. It was supposed to be cheese and tomato, and it had to have been made a week ago. Soggy doesn't begin to describe that horrible thing. I guess that's why chips (French fries) are the staple food served with just about everything you can think of. I've seen them on a pizza and as a side dish for spaghetti (I'm not kidding). Chips were cheap, filling, and available everywhere. It seemed to be the choice after a night in a pub for most. You always saw people coming out of the pubs at closing time and heading to *the chippy* as it is called.

Anyway, we spent the evening walking around. If you have the legs and enough time, you can see most of the major sights in one big walk. You can start at Piccadilly Circus—very popular with tourists. They used to say, and may still say for all I know, that if you sat there long enough, you will see everyone you know. Didn't do the test. Anyway, you start at Piccadilly, walk down Haymarket, and you come to Trafalgar Square. What a sight that is for a person who didn't even know it existed. You have the National Gallery (an art museum) to the one side, St Martin-in-the-Fields (which is a church) on the other. It's one of my favourite squares in London (apart from the stupid pigeons). They sell bird food to the tourists so the birds can shit even more. Dirty birds. I hate them. Sort of north and in between Piccadilly and Trafalgar Square stands Leicester Square where the famous Odeon Theatre has red-carpet events for movies. You continue down Whitehall (magnificent wide street and very regal looking) and you hit Big Ben and Houses of Parliament. Another sight to behold. Beside Parliament is Westminster Abbey. If your legs hold out, you can then go back up toward Trafalgar and walk very royally down the mall with St. James Park on the left up to Green Park and Buckingham Palace. As I write this, I can see all these sights quite clearly, and I miss living there.

We of course didn't do all of that in one go, but we did end up meeting a guy who ran a commune. His self-given name was Justice, and he liked Lynn. I thought he was a lowlife and a creep, so of course Lynn invited him back to our place. He was so dirty that his pores were black. She let him have a bath.

"You better clean up after him and clean it good," I told her.

All I got back was a dirty look. She was into all this hippy commune crap.

Not me, man! The bathtub that the eight of us shared was BLACK. Guess who cleaned it?

Chapter Five

I SETTLED INTO LIFE AT Fortescue House. We had a landlord called Abdul—we called him Abdoman for short. He was VERY interested in all of our comings and goings, i.e. two girls living with all these guys. Most nights (after the pub) these guys, and sometimes some of their friends, ended up in our room playing cards, strumming the guitar, talking and generally hanging out. Trust me, we had no sex or drugs, just rock and roll. At one point, we had nine guys in our room with three of them playing guitars. What a riot it was!

It was then Abdul walked in. He ordered us to leave, but we stood our ground for the time being. He really wanted us to leave though, calling us savages and ranting and raving about me and Andy. I would take him down a cup of tea in the morning. Why do women do this? Andy would never bring me a cup even if asked. To be fair, he didn't ask me to do this, I just did. So, after a couple of weeks having fun and getting along with everyone, we were thrown out and once again had no place to live. The guys next door said we could sleep on their floor until we found somewhere else. JOY! Sneaking in and out of the house without "Abdul the Asshole" (his new nickname) catching us.

I would really miss this place a lot. It was my introduction to British life, even though it really was a shit hole to live in. And even though most of the guys weren't even British.

I sure got to learn how very important pubs are to the Englishman. Pub is short for public house. I didn't know this for a long time. The guys next door had been in London the same length of time as we had but hadn't seen anything or been anywhere in the city. Just work, food, pub—that's all they knew.

Later I learned a lot of the men drinking every night were married with families. Being married didn't change the way they lived. They still did exactly what they wanted. Just like John's girlfriend waiting all week for some attention. I guess a quick screw in the back of her Mini is attention of sorts. I later found out a lot of their wives were given housekeeping money to support the family on. If they wanted more, they had to get a job. Their husbands did whatever they wanted to do. I found this concept foreign, although I don't know why because that's exactly how my father treated my mother. Let's face it, they were all alcoholics and never went without a drink. When they say an Englishman's home is the pub, they don't think about their families at home while they drink their paycheques away. Some of these guys can drink eight to ten pints of beer a night. That's a lot of money.

Enough of that. I just wanted you to get the true picture not some trumped up one so you can see what really happens.

Meanwhile, during all this being thrown out of where I lived, I had full-time 9–5 job. Talk about being thrown into life in Britain fast. I really didn't know what to expect. Well, what a blast work was. To get from Parson's Green to Blackfriars took about an hour on the tube. So, I was up at seven every morning whether or not we had been down to the pub the night before. I still took Andy his tea—and still had no idea why except that he was gorgeous and liked me (even though he had a girlfriend). I was the one working, and he was only a student seeing how much sleep he could get. I would get "many thanks" a lot from him.

I worked for Brooke Bond (through PD Bureau, the temp agency). I had time sheets the company signed, and I took them to the Bureau to get paid once a week. I made about £18 a week at 10/6 per hour, so I wasn't short of money. Brooke Bond was just down the street from St. Paul's Cathedral. My friend Jackie (a girl I worked with at the same table) would take me there on our lunch hour to listen to the choir and eat our lunches. I think that people forget that it's a church as well as a famous London landmark.

I was in heaven and loved every minute of my life. Jackie became my good friend. She was a Cockney who lived in Brockley, south east London. It was curious how I tried to fit in and became a Londoner. I think my Canadian accent might have been a giveaway. I was just a very small girl living in a very big city.

The job was typing invoices on this ancient typewriter. It was massive with invoices coming up from the floor to the typewriter. One got really strong arms moving this thing around. I was used to an IBM new machine which didn't move at all. It had a little ball inside which did all the moving. I used to complain a lot, but that got me nowhere.

The worse part of the job was the cold. Nobody had central heating even in offices. The dampness of the cold got into your body and never ever left. They took pity on me and got me my own heater. I was a very good worker and worked rings around the others.

"Must be nice" and "OK for some people" were comments I got, mostly in fun. Everyone else was used to the damp coldness that we had to work in. Most of them said they didn't want central heating, claiming it to be just a waste of money.

Well, this little heater gave me a thing called chilblains. I was typing away and looked down at my hands.

"My God!" I said to Jackie. "Look at my fingers." They were swollen to double their size.

"Oh, that's chilblains," she replied. "We don't get it because we aren't stupid enough to put our hands right up to a heater."

I'll tell you, my hands were very sore and stiff, but I still had to do my job which was typing using those very sore fingers. Everyone thought it was a great laugh. As I said, I worked rings around these people, and they didn't like it. The one who finished all her invoices first got to sort out the next lot. It was always me. Jackie spent more time smoking than she did typing.

Once, when I had so much time on my hands, the boss asked me to start adding up the invoices. What a disaster!!!! I'm sure my adding up was right, but I didn't convert the pennies to shillings, nor the shillings to pounds. I just had three columns of very high numbers. How was I to know there were twenty shillings in a pound and twelve pennies in a shilling??? No wonder the country got with the programme and now have one hundred pence to one pound. Well, that little mistake knocked me back along with my ever-growing ego. Serves me right. Don't give an important job to a foreigner, eh? They never did it again, and I stuck to typing after that.

Wow! They had this great canteen. I was very skinny. If we weren't out and about at lunchtime, Jackie and I would eat there. That's when I learned that English people eat with their fork upside down, using their knife to shove the food onto the fork.

"Boy, you eat weird" was my observation to Jackie.

"Well, I've watched you chasing those peas around on your plate for a while now without catching any" was her reply. She had a point.

As well as the canteen, they had a tea lady who came around to you in the morning. I would get tea and a buttered roll. I imagine we paid for them, but it would've been very cheap.

It was quite something—the English and their tea. They think a cup of tea fixes everything. Trouble was that everyone took it the same way (or maybe it was just served the same way) with no sugar and lots and lots of milk. You got very strong, milky tea whether you liked it or not. I hate milk and took my tea with a little sugar and a splash of milk. Not here, I didn't. I was always so wet and cold from walking from the tube station that I would drink anything that was hot.

In all the time I lived in London, I never ever owned an umbrella. I don't know why. I certainly got wet a lot and had a continual cold. You got used to having wet, snotty tissues in your shirt sleeve. You couldn't get away from the damp. In bed, the sheets felt wet as if someone had poured water on them. You got fully dressed to go to bed and put hot water bottles in which did nothing to get rid of the cold or damp.

Chapter Six

LYNN FOUND A NEW PLACE for us to live. It was off Sheppard's Bush Road and called Melrose Place. It was a nicer place than Fortescue House. We had a separate bedroom and a kitchen—not that I saw much of it as I was working all the time.

Lynn was, of course, seeing and sleeping with that guy Justice. As well as a black bathtub, he gave us all an another present. We ALL got head lice from him. It was disgusting. I had dreams about bugs running up and down my long hair. We all had to have the treatment, and of course, we all did. What a dose of reality I was living in. No heat, rain all the time, people obsessed with booze and screwing, and now head lice. I still loved it there.

One night, Lynn and I decided to treat ourselves and go out for a meal. Not fish and chips, a real dinner in a restaurant. We found one near BBC studios in Sheppard's Bush. What a cool place. Lots of stars ate there. We saw pictures of them. Lulu, Cliff Richards . . . can't remember them all. There were photos all over the walls.

"I think I'm pregnant," Lynn told me.

"What! Are you kidding me?" I couldn't believe my ears.

You must remember that in 1969, you didn't just go get an abortion if you wanted to. The birth control pill was just getting started as well. Guess Justice didn't believe in safe sex.

Lynn was crying. "What am I going to do?"

I really didn't know what to say—she couldn't marry this creep. I just let her babble on, and it made her feel a lot better. Now I knew why she wanted to go out to dinner with me. Mostly, she ignored me while hanging out with Justice. Now she needed some advice, and I had none to give her. God, how could she hang around with him, never mind let him screw her? Look what that got her. She could have told me this at home and not spoilt the one nice dinner in a long time.

The other thing I remember about that dinner was dessert. The English are big on sweets, any kind. Biscuits (cookies) are a must with a cup of tea. Well, I had a piece of pie with custard. It was superb. I was never a sweet eater, but this was different. The custard wasn't all that sweet, just really good.

A few weeks later, Lynn told me that she wasn't pregnant. No explanation at all. She did, however, go on the birth control pill, so I assumed sex would continue with that loser.

It was getting on toward the end of October. A very strange thing started to happen. You would see little kids dragging around a dummy dressed up in old clothes. They would say "penny for the guy, miss" to you. Before we knew what it was all about, we just told them to bugger off. They were collecting money for Guy Fawkes Day which is November 5th. This is known as bonfire night. They used to buy fireworks with the money people gave them to set their dummies on fire and start a big bonfire.

Guy Fawkes was one of the men who tried to kill the king in 1605. Their plan, called the gunpowder plot, was to set a few kegs of gunpowder underneath Westminster Palace on November 5th, 1605. They had thirty-six barrels of gunpowder in place, and Guy Fawkes was to do the lighting of the fuse. But someone finked, and the cellars were stormed on the night of November 4th. Guy Fawkes was arrested. The rest of the group were caught and publicly executed. So, on November 5th, the people of London lit bonfires to celebrate this failure and that the king was still alive.

One afternoon, a small boy did this thing to Lynn and I.

"Penny for the guy, miss."

Just then, another boy jumped in from nowhere and said not to give him any money as he didn't really have a guy. We felt sorry for the pair of them and gave them both some change.

"Go and have some fun and make a great big fire for us."

They laughed and ran off.

You have to know that there was no Halloween in England then. I thought they would have clued in earlier as the kids are very big on sweets. They only started celebrating Halloween recently. Apparently, it now outshines bonfire night. Go figure, the Brits.

I was in the kitchen that year on November 5th and could see all the bonfires in all the backyards around Melrose Place. It was quite a sight, and I was glad I had bothered to learn what it was all about.

I really did miss Fortescue House with everyone coming to our room at night for some fun and some tea, and beer thrown in for good measure. Even though I now lived quite some distance away, I did hang out with the guys quite a bit.

One Saturday, I went with Pete to Petticoat Lane to do some shopping. It was a cool market. I remember buying a new dress and a pair of shoes. I asked for a size five, and the guy got out these massive shoes. Apparently, in Britain, I'm a two.

I got into the habit of going to Hyde Park Corner and Speakers' Corner on a Sunday morning with whoever would go with me. What a laugh that was. Never seen so many people thinking the world was about to end. Anyone could stand on a box, railing, or whatever, and yell or speak about whatever they wanted. What a crazy way to spend a few hours.

Hyde Park was this great big park in the centre of London. London has a lot of green space—seems like every little part has its own green. Once, after Speakers' Corner, Lynn and I got tired and sat on what looked like deck chairs. Some guy came along and wanted money for us to sit on them. We moved fast, and from then on, sat on the ground. If you could, that is, because a lot of the grass had a sign on it to say you couldn't walk on it.

One Saturday (and I don't really know how this happened), Lynn and Justice took me to a commune he ran. What a bunch of dropouts and layabouts they all were. Small kids and babies, half-naked and filthy dirty, wandering about with the adults looking stoned out of their tiny little minds. They sure practiced what they preached, and I guess it's what they called "free love." Poor little kids. I couldn't stay, and so I left. I couldn't stomach anymore of this free love, flower power crap anymore. Lynn thought this was all marvelous.

"Don't you think this is great?" she'd often say while we were in that horrible place.

"No, I don't."

Those were my parting words. I never went back.

At Melrose Place, we had a bunch of male students living upstairs. I used to visit some nights. They didn't have money to drink every night like the guys at Fortescue House. It was just some place for me to go so I could get away from Lynn and Justice.

I didn't really like living at Melrose Place. The clocks had gone back, so it got dark very early. My new tube station was now Hammersmith to Blackfriars. Of course, I never wanted to shop or cook, so most nights I picked up something and chips. The something was usually chicken. I didn't really like the fish there. It had bones in it. I would take my takeout and go home to eat all by myself. Lynn was never there anymore, and I didn't really want to be involved with the guys upstairs.

Then one night, everything changed. I woke up with a guy sleeping next to me in my bed.

"Get out, you asshole!" I screamed at the unknown man.

"OK, take it easy" came the sleepy reply.

Lynn and Justice had moved the commune into my flat, sans enfants, thankfully.

"God damn it, guys. What's going to happen when the landlady finds out?"

"Don't think she will."

"Of course she will. There's only supposed to be two of us living here, not ten!" I screamed at them.

"Only for a short time until we find another place," Justice spoke up.

Well, I had no choice but to put up with them. I couldn't call the cops—squatters had rights, apparently. And I sure couldn't physically move them. Luckily, I went to work everyday, so I got some relief. They wanted ME to rent them a TV so they had something to do all day. It was November and miserable as shit outside. They really couldn't understand why I wouldn't. This didn't continue very long. For a start, there wasn't anywhere for any of them to sleep. And none of those losers were going to sleep with me. I was SO miserable.

Then one day, they all buggered off. Thank God. But then I had another problem. Lynn went with them, and I was on my own. I couldn't afford the rent by myself and was told to find someone else to share with. How was I supposed to do that? To afford my rent, I worked all day, every day. I looked in the papers but found no one. Did I really want to share with a stranger? Didn't think so.

Boy did it get real fast. The landlady's husband accused me of taking the metre money. We had to feed money into a metre to get electricity. Well, I wasn't guilty. I told them who stole their money and to call the cops. They weren't getting anything from me. After much screaming and threatening, they agreed it had nothing to do with me. They knew it the whole time, they were just trying to get more money out of me. So, I was homeless again as I couldn't afford to live there by myself.

The same landlady said I could rent a bed from her in another house she owned down the street and around the corner. I guess that was all I could afford by myself, so I agreed. I'd only been in London a short while, and this was my third place to live in. This place didn't really have a name, so I'll call it the landlady's house as that's where her and her family lived.

When she said *a bed,* that's exactly what she meant. I got a single bed and a chair. It was a huge room with about five beds in it. One other bed looked occupied. I looked around and saw men's underwear hanging up to dry and evidence of a man being there. I raced downstairs. The landlady's family lived in that house.

"You've put me in with a man!" I screamed at her.

"No, no, no" came her answer. "She young girl." The landlady's English wasn't very good. I guessed she came from Eastern Europe somewhere. She had a weasley looking excuse of man for a husband. "She be back soon, you see."

Needless to say, her words didn't give me much comfort. I went to sleep to try and get over my shock and forget my predicament. When I awoke, sure enough, there was a very butch young girl about my age sitting on her bed and looking at me. We started talking, and it turned out she wasn't really a lesbian—more of a female who wanted to be, and thought she was, a man. She sure dressed like a man. She told me she wanted a sex change operation and that her brother had the same problem. I wondered what her mom was taking while pregnant. Seemed like a very large coincidence that both siblings were born the wrong sex. None of my business, and I certainly didn't say anything to her. We actually got along OK, and when she found out I was straight, she left me alone. She had a girlfriend anyway. Being gay or trans or whatever in the 1960s wasn't accepted as normal as it is today. There was shame in her manner. She went her way, and I went mine.

As I said, the room we lived in was a large one. Trouble was there was a small electric heater that seemed to eat our money without giving off much heat. We couldn't afford to keep it going. Close your eyes and try to imagine the coldest you've ever been in your life, then pour cold water all over yourself, go to bed and try to sleep. The damp was all throughout the room—no escaping it. The single-paned windows streamed water with the condensation. So, you got dressed to go to bed. I had a couple of hot water bottles, but I could only fill them with hot water from the tap. I had no kettle.

And of course, I had nothing to distract me. No TV, radio, or record player, and just like the umbrella, it never occurred to me to buy some comfort to make my life a little bit easier. I don't really know why this never occurred to me, as any of those things would have helped my situation a great deal. Guess I was just too cheap to spend the money on myself.

So, I tended to spend the least amount of time I could there, wouldn't you? My friend Jackie from work was really good to me. I would go out with her and sometimes her cousin to this pub near where she lived with a live band. They were very good. We would split a minicab back to hers, and I would sleep on the couch. It was freezing in her mom's living room, as of course, I wasn't allowed to turn on the heat. But it was so nice to have another friend after Lynn buggered off on me.

I suppose Jackie was typical of her class. Her parents lived in Brockley, southeast London, and had a nice house. Her dad worked away from home, so I rarely saw him, but I liked her mom. She was an older version of Jackie.

Jackie chain-smoked. I mean her fingers were yellow from it as were her teeth. Even while working, she would smoke.

Before, during, and after typing invoices. She had a lot of sex and didn't seem to care with whom she slept. I was always amazed at this. To me, sex went with marriage, or at least, sex was with someone you knew a bit. With my parents' marriage the way it was, I was determined not to get knocked up and come home with a big belly. I think Jackie thought I was a prude, but I didn't care.

"Loosen up a bit and have some drinks," she'd always say to me when we were at the pub.

I would have a bit to drink but not a lot as there was a lineup of guys ready to screw the drunk me. Seemed like if you slept around, you were a slag—English for slut—although, they used the word slut too. If you didn't put out, you were a lesbian. Of course, females couldn't win either way, so why play that game?

Anyway, this wasn't how Jackie felt, and her morals were none of my business. Except for one night. She had just shared Chinese food with this guy. He was from the pub and married.

"I guess your wife and kids are eating chips for their dinner while you spend all your money on Jackie!" I screamed at him. "See you later, Jackie, after you've screwed this loser."

I was so angry it felt like someone had punched me in the belly hard. I didn't see Jackie for a long time after that.

Chapter Seven

I GUESS BY NOW IT would've been late November or early December. I sincerely wish I would have kept up my diary—no excuse why not.

I started working my lunch hour so I could get off before it was too dark. I was walking home one evening and I met someone I liked just walking down the street. His name was Barry. He was an accountant and we became friends—boyfriend and girlfriend in as much as he took me out to movies and the odd pub. I wouldn't call it the great romance of the century. All we did was kiss. To me, it was like kissing my brother, but he was company, and he did take me out.

Having a bath at the landlady's house was a real treat. I think it was the family's bathtub I used as it was all by itself in a small room. You had to pay for hot water, of course, but the thing was that there was no heat in the room. So, to get the room even warm enough to strip off and have a bath, you had to steam it up by filling the bath with only hot water. Then you had to wait until the water had cooled off enough for you to jump in. Needless to say, you didn't have a bath every day. The English never seemed to bathe at all. A common comment I heard the English say was "I have a bath once a week whether I need one or not." With all this hassel about hot water and no heat, it's no wonder. I could never have a bath at Jackie's house. She just used to spray smelly stuff all over herself instead.

But I'm sure this bath at home was a specially rigged one so the landlord could watch the occupant naked. I always had this feeling of being watched. This man was a creep. He was always walking into my room without knocking whenever he pleased, and he caught me half-dressed a few times. The room didn't lock. He gave me the creeps, and I felt so sorry for his mouse of a wife who I'm sure put up with a lot of shit.

Jackie and her fellow of the day would sometimes go out with Barry and me. It didn't happen very often because the pub she liked was lively and swinging, not like the quiet, boring ones Barry took us to.

I still went on occasion to Fortescue House just to check in, but everyone was leaving. Tacus and Pete would keep me company, but they both were moving on.

Barry would take me to a double show on a Saturday night. I think that was because we could still be out on a date but not have to talk to each other. Every single Saturday night, the landlord would lock the door, and I had to bang to get in.

Well, I was getting sick of this so-called relationship. I knew I was lonely, but this was not really filling any gap in my life. I knew nothing about him, not even where he lived or worked.

"Why can't we do something fun like dancing or go to Jackie's pub where there's live music?" I would ask.

"Not really what I like" was his dismissive reply.

No thought that maybe I was bored and needed more than a movie once a week. I remembered John (the original one from Fortescue House) and how he liked to only take his girlfriend out once a week. Maybe this is the way the English treated their wives/girlfriends. So, I started to cancel these outings and soon saw less and less of Barry. I was better off by myself.

Turns out, I guess Barry liked/loved me more than I did him. I came home one night to find that he had redecorated my space. He had written "Iloveyou" (just like that) all over my stuff and left love letters for me. He even wrote on my hot water bottle. I wasn't scared—yet.

Next thing I knew, he had moved into the small room right next door.

"Why didn't you stop him!?" I yelled at my roommate. Now I was getting scared.

"None of my business" came her reply.

Of course, all the landlady wanted was his money, so she didn't care. I was screwed. Now, I couldn't go back to my room. I didn't know him at all, so I didn't trust what he would do next.

I ended up living between Jackie's and Fortescue House, but most of my stuff was still in my room at the landlady's house. I was scared to go get the rest of my things.

It was on one of my trips to Fortescue House that I saw Lynn again. Justice and his gang had spent all her money and dumped her, so she was back. She was living with a guy called Dennis—one of the Aussies who had lived downstairs when I lived there. His friend John had left and Lynn had moved in. She had a job as a tea lady (she didn't take typing in school).

"Well, what a surprise to see you again," she said to me but didn't really seem interested in my life so far.

I suspect she was embarrassed about being used that way by Justice and his crew.

"Can I spend a few nights here?" I asked after I explained the situation I had found myself in again.

"Sure can" came Dennis' reply, a little too fast.

I had always thought he was a bit of a snake, but I had to sleep somewhere. Even though I didn't go home, I still had to pay the rent. I couldn't afford to rent anywhere else. Besides, I didn't have time to look for a new place, and I was scared to go and get the rest of my things.

So, Lynn and Dennis were living together. He didn't work but lived off her wage as a tea lady. Boy could she ever pick them—another freeloader sponging off her. Again, she didn't seem to mind.

"I'm screwing a dancer as well as Lynn," Dennis bragged to me one night after having too many beers.

"My friend is supporting you, paying your rent, feeding you, and you're cheating on her? I gather she doesn't know." I doubted Lynn would've cared.

"No, she doesn't and don't go telling her, will you?"

"None of my business. Just don't go and get any of them pregnant. There's a good boy."

Dennis didn't care about sarcasm or shots thrown his way. He was just a guy out to get as much sex as he could, and there were always females ready to oblige him in his quest.

I was of two minds whether to tell Lynn or not. She shouldn't have had to put up with this shit from a creep like Dennis, but she had left me in the crapper on more than one occasion. *So, I thought, screw it, let her find out herself.* Totally not like me at all, and I still regret not telling her. She most probably knew—most women do—but just put up with the stupid bastard.

I started sleeping on the floor at the foot of their bed instead of beside Lynn. They had put the two beds together so I kind of had my own bed. But they always had sex beside me, so I made my bed the floor, and I sure was getting sick of the arrangement.

Once when Dennis tried it on, she said, "You can't, there's something else in there tonight." (She had her period.)

Poor Dennis had to go without. Never mind, there was always the dancer tomorrow. When they did manage to have sex, there was no kissing, foreplay, or any kind of affection on his part. The dick went straight in and banged away until he came. Then he went to sleep. Hard work that.

"Why do you put up with this crap?" I would ask Lynn. "You mustn't get anything out of him screwing you at all."

"I don't. It mostly just hurts. I don't know why I let him do it to me. I guess because he expects it."

"Christ, if that's what sex is like, I'm glad I don't have any. Are you still on the pill?"

"Oh yea! I'm not going through that again."

I vowed to change this situation—staying here was no longer an option for me. Time to find somewhere else to live once again.

So how to proceed? I couldn't keep sleeping on people's floors and couches. Nor could I afford another place as long as I paid rent at the landlady's house.

I talked it out with Jackie; she was about the only person left who could be objective. She didn't really care what I did but was good enough to help me out. We decided to go back to where all my stuff was and check it out. She came with me. I couldn't just call the landlady to see if Barry was still there because I didn't know what her number was, or even if she had a phone. I never thought I'd have to call her.

Barry had gone. There was no reason for him to stay since I was gone. I'm sure his place was a lot nicer than the bed next door to me. What a relief I could stay there awhile until I figured out my next move. Besides, Christmas was coming.

Without all the hassels I had the last little while, going back to work was a treat. Always in the back of my mind was that Barry would show up sooner or later, but he never did.

On a Friday, Jackie and I would use our lunch to go get our paycheques from PD Bureau. To get to Shaftesbury Avenue (where PD Bureau was), you could walk past 10 Downing Street—the home and offices of the prime minister of the day and just a few minutes walk to the Houses of Parliament. Downing Street wasn't blocked off then as it is now. There were no barriers—nothing to stop you going down that magnificent short street.

December in London was mild by Canadian standards, of course, but the damp and lack of sun and indoor heat made it seem way worse even when it wasn't raining. That winter, it snowed in London quite a bit. I loved it. It was that wet, yucky snow not good for much, so I threw a snowball at Jackie. She was not impressed, called me names, and the snow wrecked her eye makeup. She had two black eyes. Not a good sport at all. I was only trying to have some fun that didn't involve getting drunk, smoking or sleeping around—three of her favourites.

Christmas came, and her mom invited me over to spend it with them. What a treat! The first proper home cooking I'd had since leaving home in September (or even before that). Her mom was a good cook, and this table had everything. A ham, a turkey, several kinds of potatoes, vegetables, stuffing and cranberries. I can still taste how good it was. So, some English people could cook—who knew? It was a great family day for me, and I appreciated it a lot. We even exchanged gifts. I think I was a novelty to them—someone different to learn about.

They introduced me to this Irish guy called John. I don't think the man worked at all. A lot of Irish would come to England and go on the dole. But he was nice enough and took me out with Jackie and her friend of the day. I always paid my own way and never ever drank too much. He was my date for a New Year's Eve party her parents had. It was the first time I had spent any time with Jackie's father. He was a lovely hardworking man. I can't remember what his job was though.

Anyway, I got a little tipsy that night. I think John helped me along thinking if I got drunk enough, I'd sleep with him. I remember standing at the top of the stairs and calling to Jackie's dad.

"Come and catch me, I'm going to jump!"

Someone grabbed me and laid me down on the couch (the same couch I'd slept on a million times before).

In the morning, I got quite a shock.

"What do you mean we have to go work today? It's New Year's Day for God's sake."

"I know, we work on New Year's Day over here," Jackie informed me.

"What a stupid idea. I wish you would've told me because I wouldn't have drunk so much."

"Never mind, get dressed, we're going to be late."

Off we went to work.

I went out with this Irish John a few more times, always with Jackie and her boyfriend of the day, but I made them do things I liked to do. We went ten-pin bowling even though I had only ever done five-pin. The balls were heavy. The guys were OK because, of course, they sold beer there, so the bowling was secondary. Then I dragged them ice skating—not a popular English pastime as you can imagine. I had a ball. I can't recall if any of them had the balls to even try. I didn't care; it beat drinking and smoking in a pub to me. Funny though that after these outings, nobody would let me plan any more trips out. I finally got bored with this guy who wasn't really up to much, and we stopped going out altogether. I still saw Jackie and her many friends.

Sometime in January, we all got the bad news. We were being replaced by computers at Brooke Bond, so were all out of work. I remember my boss called me in to tell me himself. He thought we were great buddies because he'd been to Niagara Falls (the Canadian side).

"Sorry we have to let you go, but computers are the future. You should have no problem getting another job. You're a very good worker."

That wasn't it at all. It was just that I worked instead of smoking, going to the loo, or talking like the rest of them did continually.

Chapter Eight

SO, NOW I LIVED IN a scary place with a lesbian and an ex-boyfriend who could come and harass me at anytime. And now I was unemployed. Luckily, I had quite a lot of money saved. You don't spend much when you work all day and go to bed early every night.

I was quite sure I could get a new job anytime I needed one, but having some time off could be fun for awhile. Maybe I could do some more sightseeing. I could visit museums and all the tourist spots I hadn't seen because I was always working. I hadn't even been to the Tower of London yet. And winter was a good time to see the sights in London as most of the tourists had gone home—couldn't hack the lovely weather, I guess.

Hold that thought. Too good to be true again. I caught a cold to end all colds (may even have been the flu, I was that sick). I mean, I'd had sniffles the whole time I lived in London (comes with the city) but I never missed a day's work. Man, was I ever sick. No one was going to bring me any chicken soup or even come see if I was alive or dead. Jackie knew but wanted no part. She didn't want to get ill as well.

So, I stayed in my single bed, feeling cold, damp and alone, and I slept. Never during this time did it cross my mind I could just go home. Home—where I could have a HOT bath, where there was heat in my house, where someone might give a shit if I lived or died. Do I sound like I felt sorry for myself? I don't think I did. I was too sick. I just slept day and night for I don't know how long.

Finally, one day, Jackie came to see if I were still alive. I think she brought me food as I wasn't eating or drinking very much. My landlady was only interested in the £4/week she got for my rent. By the time Jackie came, I was feeling a bit better. She had found me a new place to live.

"Where do I have to go now?" I pondered over some new dump.

"Do you remember Miriam and Yvonne from work?"

"Vaguely, I don't think I actually worked with either of them. Weren't they on a few tables down from us?"

"They were. I was talking to Miriam the other day, and she has a spare room she'll rent to you. It's in a proper house, and you'll have use of the kitchen if you want. She seems like a nice person. Yvonne is actually her sister. What do you think?"

"Sounds good to me. Anything to get out of here before Barry finds out I'm back here."

She gave me Miriam's home phone number, and I rang her to finalize plans to move in. She lived on Denmark Hill which was southeast London, just down from Camberwell Green. I took the place sight unseen. I was just happy to be around people again.

We made plans for the following weekend. Luckily, Jackie was free. Her and I had all my junk in plastic bags, my small suitcase, and anything else we could shove stuff into. Thank God for Jackie. I would've had to have made at least two trips by myself. As it was, we made it in one go. She knew the way, so I just followed along. We took the tube to Elephant and Castle and then a couple of buses to Miriam's place.

I could give this more permanent address to my guys back home, and maybe, just maybe, someone would actually write me back.

The room I had was large enough and on the top floor. One flight down was the toilet in its own little room. I still had a single bed, but that's all I needed. I had a wardrobe to actually hang my clothes up in. I remember the room wasn't as damp and cold as the one I had just left. I suppose the heat from downstairs rose up to my room, keeping me warm. There was a bathtub in the kitchen. Never had I seen that before, but at least it had hot water I didn't have to pay for. The rent was the same £4, and she said I could eat dinner with them as she had to cook for her two teenage girls anyway. WOW!!!!!!!! A free dinner thrown in to top it off. What a deal. Plus, this place was a lot closer to where Jackie lived. I actually had a key to the front door, and it seemed like a really nice place to live.

And so, I settled in. I figured I should go get some groceries for other meals and my tea etc. It was just amazing what £1 could buy you. I was checking out and had paid for my groceries. The cashier just left it in a heap. I looked at her.

"Where are your carrier bags?" she asked me.

"What are carrier bags?"

"You need them to carry your groceries home in."

"Don't you provide bags?"

"Nope."

She was getting snarky—probably thought I was an American by my accent and lack of carrier bags. She needed my stuff moved.

I just stood there looking stupid when someone gave me a box. I packed my things and went home. Luckily, it wasn't a far walk.

Large grocery stores weren't around there then, and they had more specialty shops i.e. green grocery, meat guy, sweet shop etc. Most English women would shop daily, and a lot of them didn't have a fridge, so that worked out well.

Miriam had a fridge and I could keep my stuff in it. It was nice to have my own food and to cook a bit. I got used to the bath being there as well.

They had a living room with a TV in it which I was allowed to use. What a treat. I think it was the first time I'd seen TV since I left Canada. Mind you, I think they only got three or four stations, but I didn't care. I'd watch anything just to be out of my room. I did love being around people again and realized how lonely I had been.

Miriam had two teenage girls who lived there and a son called Roy who was away at boarding school in Norfolk. She seemed to do alright for someone who only worked part-time and was divorced. I never knew if she rented or owned the house, and of course, once again, it was none of my business. I was just happy not to be by myself anymore.

Even the location of Miriam's didn't upset me. It was SE London, but with the buses and the tube, you could go anywhere quite quickly.

You've never lived until you've been on a double-decker bus. Back then, the backs were open so you could jump on. The drivers had a cool trick they did—waited until you had grabbed the bar and then took off like bats out of hell. It nearly separated your shoulder from your arm. It happened too often for it not to be planned. Then, of course, you walked up the spiral stairs to the top floor where you could smoke (not that I smoked, but you got the best view up there).

You must remember this was the age of the miniskirt, so onlookers saw quite a few ladies' crotches (and I mean mine too). I rarely wore tights, but I did have knickers on, so the view was pretty good. Never even crossed my mind, and I wouldn't have minded anyway. If my crotch gave some guy a thrill, so what? Great for him.

All the driver did was drive. He had his own little cab to sit in. If you've ever seen the UK TV series *On the Buses*, you'll know what I mean. Then they had a conductor who had a machine which whipped out the tickets. You told him where you were going, and he gave you a ticket out of this machine he wore around his neck. Imagine the abuse that went on. English people always seemed to be on some kind of fiddle. It was always an interesting ride. It was also a great way to see London without walking. Just sit on top and in the front and sightsee away.

So here I was living in a nice place in a nice area with nice people. The weather was getting warmer and a bit less rainy. Instead of spending the rest of my money, I decided I was well enough to go back to work.

I went to PD Bureau and was sent to a new place to work. I didn't really think much about it at the time, but it was a very posh place. It was next door to the Mayfair Hotel, across the road from Green Park (the park) and Green Park (the tube station). I took several tries at finding the quickest and most direct route to get there from Denmark Hill.

On my first day, I showed up to work and was taken to my room downstairs. I can't exactly remember what I had to do, but it couldn't have been very taxing because I was finished by lunchtime. I emerged to say I was done to astonished looks.

"It took the girl before you all day to do that job," one of the ladies said.

"Well, I'm done and need something else to do for the afternoon."

They were all very nice to me and suggested I take a lunch break. I suppose so they could figure out what else I could do.

So off I went to get a sandwich. It was a lovely area with nice buildings and a great looking park to eat in. I grabbed something to eat and took it over to Green Park to eat it. *Boy, this is the life,* I thought. *Having lunch in a park with no rain, waiting for people to find me work to do.*

When I returned a bit later, they were ready for me.

"We'd like you to keep doing what you did this morning, but in the afternoons you can come up here and give us a hand," the lady who seemed to run everything informed me.

"OK by me" was my stupid reply. "As long as I keep busy, I don't care what I do."

So that's how it went. Mornings were spent downstairs (stuffing envelops, I think) for clients. And in the afternoons, I was upstairs answering phones and giving clients the correct information packets they needed. It was sort of a job centre place where clients would call to inquire about a certain job, and we would mail them the job info. That was the first time I heard the word esquire. Instead of Mr. John Smith, you put John Smith Esq. I thought it was very posh indeed.

Well, the whole setup was posh. In the morning, coffee was served instead of tea. I HATE coffee, so they gave me milk instead of tea. As you well know, I HATE milk as well. I started getting takeaway tea and toast on my way to work in the mornings. You also got tea and biscuits (cookies) in the afternoon. Work started at 9:30 a.m. and finished at 5:30 p.m. with an hour for lunch (for which I didn't get paid). The three ladies who worked upstairs were very nice to me. They saw me as a very little girl trying to fit into a very large lifestyle in a very large city. They didn't treat me like a kid, and I was grateful for that. They were all middle-aged and probably had kids my age themselves, and so I suppose they wanted to look out for me. I liked all three and really loved my work there. I also got to know the area very well by going for walks at lunchtime.

I still saw Jackie some weekends, but because I lived that much closer, I came home at night. We mostly went to that one pub, and I was very careful not to drink much. I didn't want a repeat of New Year's Eve. There was a pub full of guys who would take advantage of any drunk girl. If I was going to have sex, I wasn't about to be raped or not remember because I was drunk. I did like the pub Jackie and I went to. It usually had live music on a Saturday night (which is when we tried to go). I don't think we had the chance to dance because there were too many people crowded together trying to see the band perform.

You need to know that the guys over there were very macho, treating women as if they were there for their sole use. Nobody treated me that way. I wouldn't let them. In fact, a few were friends of mine. To illustrate this lack of respect for the female person, here are the names they called us: birds, crumpet, dolly birds, a bit, a bit of fluff, a piece, a piece of tail. You can see the attitude.

"I drink pints, me" would be a sentence I heard a lot.

Women didn't factor into their lives at all (including their wives). They did what they wanted, when they wanted. I learned this quickly and stayed out of their way. Wasn't interested in being my mom.

Once, when I was at Jackie's house, her cousin was getting herself all dolled up. This was something girls did before going to the pub. You had to wonder what part of them was real between wigs, false eyelashes, makeup to the nines, etc.

"What's going on?" I asked her.

"I'm planning on getting pregnant tonight."

I started to laugh but could see she was serious. "What are you talking about?"

"Well, I've been going out with this man for a while now, and I plan on having unprotected sex tonight with him to see if I can get pregnant. Just planning what to cook to get him in the mood."

"Are you kidding me? Why on earth would you think that would work? He'll just leave once he finds out you're knocked up. Why would he marry you? Having a baby won't change anything. You'll just be left with a baby to raise by yourself."

I couldn't believe she was serious. I had to leave before I got into trouble with the pair of them.

I went home not believing what I had just heard. I knew they weren't very bright, but getting pregnant deliberately to catch a man?? In what world would that work? It was a while before I went back to Jackie's. These people's lack of morals was beginning to get me down. Nobody seemed to care, but I didn't have to watch it. Maybe a lot had to do with all the booze they drank. I don't know.

I was getting sick of being called a Yank. It was an insult to me. Who wants to be called an American, especially when you are a Canadian? It wasn't the English's fault. The accents were the same to them. It didn't matter how many flags you wore on your shirt. They didn't know a Canadian one from an Italian one. The thing was though that the Brits didn't like Americans, so that caused problems at first. But when they found out I was a Canadian, attitudes changed quickly. Still, I didn't like it, and I told as many people as I could that they shouldn't assume someone with a North American accent was an American. They ought to ask where the person is from first before assuming the worst. I doubt I got through to many, but I did try.

One weekend (this must have been into March by now), I visited Fortescue House again. I hadn't been there for quite a while, not since I was hiding from Barry. Seemed like pot had found these guys while I was away. They knew my views on smoking dope and didn't do it in front of me. If anyone did, I just left.

Lynn was still in the same room with Dennis. Nothing had changed there then. Tacus was still around but looking worse for wear from the drugs. John (the original creep who had left to go home for Christmas) was back. He and Tacus were talking about getting a place with the Aussie John—Dennis' mate. Anything would be better than Fortescue House. After being away for a while, I could see how really run-down the place was.

They all asked what I was up to, and I told my story, and they told me theirs. Tacus was still in school, and John got his old job back with London Transport. I didn't ask the Aussie about himself because I didn't care.

Of course, we all ended up going to the pub to catch up. Seemed to be the only place to go, so we went. Maybe they all drank so much to forget about the weather or to get courage for their next screw. I didn't know, but drinking was always around. And now pot was here too. I knew Dennis smoked pot, so I suppose Lynn did too. Where did they get all the money to buy drugs? Guess it's always the way—there's always money for what's essential.

Actually, I had fun catching up with them. John had worked in pubs over Xmas in Hull, where he was from. Nobody knew where Pete had gone. He had given up on my being his girlfriend a long time ago. I hadn't bothered to keep in touch. I didn't want to. I would be his friend, that was all. So, our little reunion was nice, and we promised to keep in touch. Miriam had a phone, so they could call if they wanted to. It was nice to see them, except I was worried the way Lynn kept letting men use her. I wasn't a good enough friend to interfere, and I assumed she would come to me if she needed my help (like when she thought she was pregnant). People always came to me when they needed help. It was a bit of a hike to see them from Denmark Hill, so I decided if I did do it again, it'd be from work.

I got on with my life—working and loving (really *loving*) living on Denmark Hill with a family. I pulled my weight and helped out when I could. I would, of course, clean up after myself in the kitchen after cooking, and I kept my room clean. It was nice to be clean again.

They had a Wimpy's bar near Miriam's. It wasn't a bar, and I had no idea why it was called one, but it was what we would call a hamburger joint. They served the worst hamburger I'd ever eaten. You just got a patty with burnt, cooked onion on top. There was brown and red sauce on the table.

"Where's the tomato, lettuce, pickle, mustard and relish?" I asked some poor overworked guy trying to make a living selling this pathetic excuse for food.

"This isn't America" came the snotty answer. "This is England, by the way."

"You don't know what you're missing, pal. And I'm Canadian."

"Glad to hear it." He didn't give a shit.

Then he served me my strawberry milkshake. WOW! Milk with red stuff in it. I kept my mouth shut. No sense in rocking this boat anymore. After a while, you got used to this version of a meal and even came to like it. The English were not good cooks, but I was living here, so I got used to what was served to me.

Miriam could cook, and sometimes I actually was home in time for dinner but not very often. I didn't leave work until 5:30 p.m. or later, depending on what needed to be finished at work, so by the time I got home, dinner was over. Sometimes, she put a plate away for me but not very often. Chips for dinner again.

Work was going well. I fit in and got along with everyone. One day, my boss called me into her office. *Oh God, here we go again. Can a computer do this job?* I didn't think so. I also couldn't think of anything I'd done wrong, but you never know, do you? I mean, you don't see the boss for good news, do you? That's exactly what it was though, good news. They were so impressed with my work, they wanted to hire me. I would no longer work for PD Bureau but for them.

"We can't afford to pay you the same salary as the temp agency," she explained.

"How much less?" I still had to support myself, flattered as I was to be asked.

"Only a few quid a week less. But the job comes with perks like luncheon vouchers."

"What's that?"

"They are vouchers you can use for lunch when you eat out. They are worth a lot more than a few pounds a week."

I didn't need convincing. "Sounds good to me and thanks."

"You deserve to be hired, and we are glad to have you until you have to go home in September."

Until she said that, I forgot I had to go home at the end of the summer. But, until then, I had a great job with people who appreciated my work and liked me. I liked them back too.

I had bought some new clothes and stuff but apart from tube/bus fares, I mostly saved my money. I didn't really go out since I wasn't seeing Jackie and her crazy cousin or any of the guys from Fortescue House anymore.

Chapter Nine

OUT OF THE BLUE, JACKIE called Miriam's to see how I was doing. It was good to hear from her again. Although I didn't agree with her lifestyle, she had been very good to me when we worked together. So, we agreed to meet up the following Saturday night at the pub (where else?). I would've been just as happy if she came over to Miriam's and we watched TV, but of course that wasn't something that was done. You must go to the pub.

Mind you, it was the same pub with live music, and I knew some of the people there. Mostly I didn't like them. Too many of them were married men who chose to be at a pub instead of home with their families. I always wondered what kind of a woman puts up with this crap. I guess they grew up watching their fathers do the same and thought nothing wrong with this bad behaviour. I sure did, but nobody cared what I thought.

After the way my mom was treated, no man would ever treat me like that. I say that, but there I was taking tea every morning down to Andy while he slept and I had to go to work. By the way, I learned a lot later that the whole house thought I was sleeping with him. It never occurred to them that we could just be friends. I'm sure he would have tried it on if I gave him half a chance. He was only a man after all.

Why do women give way to men at every turn? Jackie slept around with anyone—why? Lynn let Dennis practically rape her. Why? Do we lack confidence in ourselves? Or are we programmed to bend to the will of a man? Don't know the answer and never will. I'm just as guilty as everyone else with the tea thing. Andy didn't ask for the tea, but I went out of my way to bring it to him. Enough of that!!!

So, I went to meet Jackie at the pub. Living at Denmark Hill, I could go home at night and not have to stay overnight at Jackie's and put her mom out. I was only a bus ride or minicab ride away. I never felt scared or even thought about travelling by myself in London the entire time I lived there.

It was nice to see her, and for once, she was by herself, so we could talk between sets of music which was too loud to talk over. I certainly didn't ask her how her love life was because I knew how it was and didn't really care. She knew how I felt, so we just didn't go there.

"My new job is great. I get luncheon vouchers with this job but less pay than PD Bureau paid us. I really like it there. I work right beside the Mayfair Hotel."

"How posh for you. I'm not working right now, but I'm planning to call PD soon and get back to work. My mom says hi and to come to see her sometime."

Of course, I can't make you hear Jackie's cool Cockney accent. I rarely heard any rhyming slang Cockneys are noted for, but sometimes it was difficult for me to understand what was being said.

"Sure, I will now that 1 live a lot closer. We'll sort out something soon."

We just listened to the band. Jackie had a "crush" on the singer. I had known about this for a long time. He was engaged to be married, but that wouldn't have stopped either one of them from screwing had he fancied her at all.

Jackie always drank more than I did. I guess because she was used to it and could hold her liquor way better than I could. There were a lineup of guys ready to nail any female who got a bit too tipsy. It sure wasn't going to be me. Anyway, I didn't really like to drink too much. I couldn't stand the taste of beer, especially English beer which could be really strong. Mind you, there were plenty of girls who drank pints.

The band took a break and the singer walked over to Jackie and me. *Wow,* I thought, *maybe he really does like her.* Nope, it was me he wanted to talk to.

"I'm done now and wondered if I could drive you home?" he asked me.

Good, a free ride home in the rain. What luck.

"OK. Come get me when you're ready to leave."

"What did he want?" Jackie demanded.

"He's going to drive me home," I said.

"Are you going to do it? That's not like you."

"It's a free ride home, and it's pouring down with rain, so I'm going to let him drive me home, OK?"

She just turned around and left without another word to me. *What's wrong with her,* I said to myself.

I can't even remember this guy's name, that's how much of an impression he made on me. We got in his van—yes, his van. I gave him my address and on we drove. We chatted all the way about nothing really (I can't remember the conversation). When he got to my place, he pulled around the corner instead of dropping me in front of the house. The penny dropped.

"You think I'm going to jump in the back of this van with you, don't you?"

"I was hoping. You let me drive you home, after all."

"Yea. For a free ride home in the rain, not for a screw in the back of your van. I thought you were getting married?"

"I am."

"What a good husband you're gonna make. How stupid can you be? I don't have sex with strangers. You should be ashamed of yourself, you pig! If that's what you were after, why didn't you take Jackie home instead of me? She likes you, and she'd give you what you are looking for. She's up for anything."

"Yea, I know. Ever hear of the song—if you want it, here it is, come and get it??"

I shook my head.

"Well, I don't want it from her."

"You're not getting it from me, that's for sure, man."

"What about a snog?"(As if I knew what a snog was.)

"What's a snog?"

"A kiss," he said with hope.

"Nope. Go back to your poor fiancée and hope she doesn't find out what a pig you are. Maybe I should tell her and save her a lifetime full of crap from you."

"You don't know who she is."

"Look, I'm not going to argue with you. I'm leaving. I think you're the worst kind of scumbag I've ever met. Do me a favour and call off your wedding. Give the girl a break."

I slammed the door and ran to my house as fast as I could. OK. OK. I know—how could I have been this stupid? Obviously, I was. I really thought I was just getting a free ride home in the rain. It never occurred to me I would have to put out in the back of a van with someone I didn't even know very well. Over the years, I've thanked my lucky stars I wasn't raped. There was no one around to stop him. You know those women who don't know they're pregnant until they pop out a baby? Well, I felt as stupid as one of them.

Who was to know the worst was yet to come. Jackie completely ignored me and wouldn't answer any of my calls. Her mom would say she'd call me back, but she never did. I guess I could take a hint. Finally.

"Please, can I talk to her, Mrs. Denham? I don't know why she won't talk to me."

"She doesn't want to talk to you, and she won't tell me why," was the reply I got.

Oh well—I guess she doesn't want me as a friend. I didn't find out why for a long time. Then, out of the blue, she called Miriam's, and I just happened to be there.

"I guess you're pleased with yourself, taking a lift from that singer."

"What are you talking about?"

"Did he give you a good time? You really are a slut and out for yourself, aren't you?" She banged down the phone and that was the end of that.

It wasn't until many many years later when it dawned on me why she was so mad at me. She assumed that I had slept with that creep, as of course she would have done. I knew she liked him, and she must have thought that I would make the same choices as her sex-wise. Although why I will never know as she knew I didn't sleep around. I didn't think that way at the time and wasn't following her logic. I never even got a chance to tell her what really happened at the time, and she may not have believed me anyway. Imagine her calling me a slut!!!!

I guess our friendship had ended—all over a guy who was a pig and planning on marrying someone else. I still feel sorry for his wife (if indeed he really did marry her, and I'm quite sure he did and continued to fool around on her).

Spring was here in London, and the weather turned quite nice (for London, not Toronto). After the winter I just had, any day it wasn't cold and rainy was a great day to me.

Work was going well, and I felt appreciated there. In fact, the boss' secretary was immigrating to the States, and I filled in for her for a while until a more permanent one could be found. If I were not going home, I'm sure the job would've been mine. I did love it. It offered me variety and responsibility, but of course, I wasn't paid any additional salary for filling in. Looking back, I often wonder if I could have applied for an extension as a visitor to a more permanent status so I could have stayed in that beautiful city a bit longer. Unfortunately, I didn't even think that way while I had the chance. It may not have been possible, but I'll never know.

I was missing my clan from Fortescue House, so one weekend, I paid them a visit. Lynn and Dennis were there, still in the same room. Both seemed glad to see me. John was there too. You know John—the creepy one who offered to let me in the first day at Fortescue House. He had asked his girlfriend to marry him, then took it back and dumped her. He had a flat with Tacus (the Greek guy) and John (the other Aussie who shared with Dennis originally).

We all started talking and got along great once again. Of course, we proceeded to the pub and had a few drinks. It was there that John—the original creep I didn't like very much—asked me out. What Englishmen mean by asking girls out is a drink at the pub followed by a guaranteed shag at the night's end. I agreed to go out with him. I hadn't been out since Jackie and that van guy incident.

But I didn't fancy drinking in a pub all night without conversation, so I suggested—well, more than suggested—we go on a real date. I picked a movie, and we said we'd meet there. I really didn't think he'd show up, but he did. The movie was *Rosemary's Baby*. Of course, we had no conversation at the show either. The movies there had no popcorn, just some lady standing in the intermission with a container full of sweets and ice cream. Very strange to me. A movie without popcorn. I suppose it was very strange for John as well. A night without booze.

Well, a good choice for a first date—a horror film, and I don't think I realized what it was about when I chose it. I remember Mia Farrow was really good acting in it, and I remember being quite scared. I wasn't into all that satanic stuff. I should've picked a comedy. I took John back to Miriam's place. I liked riding buses with him as he worked for London Transport and had a pass. When he flashed it to the conductor, he never made me pay. When I talk about fiddles, this is what I mean. They were all at it on the buses.

Back in my room, we talked for a while, mainly about the crazy movie we had just seen, and made out a little bit. With his reputation, I don't know what I was thinking bringing him back to my place. I wasn't going to put out if that's what he thought. I didn't know what to think as I had invited him back. It was like when that guy gave me a ride and expected a shag for doing so. It was time for him to go.

"I've missed my last bus."

"You can't stay here. I only have this single bed."

"We can share it. Remember when you stayed with me and Pete?"

"That was different. We slept on the floor, and Lynn was there too. I don't think we should share any beds tonight, not after that scary movie."

"It's a long walk back to my place, and I can't afford a minicab."

So, against my better judgement, he stayed. Don't remember much about it except he didn't get lucky, and I'm sure that was to his disappointment. We just slept. He knew I didn't sleep around, and if he wanted to date me, that was the way it would be. Mind you, it was strange sleeping beside someone so close to me in a single bed. I'd never done it before, and I'm quite sure he hadn't either. I hoped this wasn't going to be a regular thing.

I had known him since I arrived in London, and we had gone out as a group many times with the guys from Fortescue House. I even went on a date with him and his girlfriend. I'm sure she was thrilled with that. But because of this treatment of that girlfriend, I didn't like him that much. Why on earth was I sleeping in the same bed as him? I did come to realize it was the way British men were brought up to treat their women. Maybe that's why he liked me. He couldn't push me around. I wouldn't take any bullshit from anyone, and certainly not from men. He got sick of his former girlfriend, even though she knuckled down and did what she was told.

She must have known I went out with John when she wasn't around which was most of the time. She never said anything to me about it. I would've set her straight. I wasn't interested in her boyfriend even after they were engaged. She didn't even have the balls to tell me off. I did feel sorry for her though when he told her he couldn't marry her. What a rotten trick to pull on someone. She just turned around and walked away. Unfortunately, I was there watching and feeling sorry for her. No more Mini for John as he used to drive her Mini all the time even with her in it. Talk about taking advantage of someone. Once, he even had sex with her in his bed at Fortescue House. I know this because the guys put the door open a bit so everyone could watch. They didn't know, of course. It was not nice of them, but there you go.

We started seeing each other off and on for a while, mostly just meeting up for a few drinks. I still wasn't sure what I thought about him. In principle, I didn't like how Englishmen (and I supposed all men—I didn't know much about it) treated women. Even given the fact they seemed to be all the same, didn't matter to me. I certainly would never let any man I knew get the better of me nor control what I did. Seeing my mom being treated like dirt by my father was enough for me. Maybe all men were like this. If so, what were girls to do?

My work kept me sane. The women treated me like their daughter and looked after me by giving me somewhat uninvited advice. I didn't mind. It meant that they cared about me, which was more than I could say about a lot of people then. At the time, I didn't really appreciate the posh location I worked at. I was often too tired after work to take advantage of my location. But, sometimes, usually on a Friday night when work wasn't happening the next day, I would go for a long walk.

From Green Park, you could go on a few scenic walks and hit a lot of cool places. One walk I took went through Green Park to Buckingham Palace, then I cut up to Hyde Park Corner, and down Knightsbridge to Harrods. I just looked outside at Harrods. I didn't really want to see what I couldn't afford. What a lovely area it was, très posh and very rich. Just walking around, not really knowing what everything was all about or where the tourist things were was a big treat for me.

I loved this city.

The other walk I did the most was the other way down Piccadilly Street from Green Park tube station to Piccadilly Circus. A lot of Americans hung around there. Just down from there is Leicester Square where movies premier from, even now. Keep on walking to Trafalgar Square where you'll find Canada House on the opposite corner. It was nice to know something called Canada House was nearby. I never went in it. Usually, I'd had enough by then and headed home.

One evening, coming home from work, I had a brown envelope waiting for me from the government. This was not a good sign for someone who was an alien working in a foreign country. *It can't be good news,* I thought to myself.

"Came in the second post," I was told by Miriam.

They had two deliveries of mail in a single day in London back then. I don't really know why.

I ripped it open. Basically, it said they wanted to see me and that I hadn't been paying income tax on my paycheques. *Oh God! I'm going to be thrown in jail or the very least be kicked out of England. What am I going to do?* They wanted a lot of money that I didn't have. Of course, Miriam gave me no sympathy. She didn't really care much about my goings-on unless it effected her or her rent.

Luckily, the next day was a work day, so I took the letter to my ladies at work. Maybe someone there could help me or at least give me some sympathy.

They did more than that.

The head boss—I think she was my boss—looked at it and told me, "Don't worry, dear, my husband will sort this out for you."

Her husband will sort this out??? Easy for her to say, she wasn't in any trouble. I had no choice but to let her have the letter to try and sort the mess out for me. I certainly couldn't.

What a nerve-wracking week that was. All sorts of terrible thoughts went through my head, from being hung at the Tower of London to going to jail. Isn't it funny how guilty you are made to feel even though you don't know what you did wrong?

Turns out PD Bureau was at fault. Although they deducted income tax from my paycheque, they kept the money for themselves and didn't report it to the government. I guess they thought all these foreigners would be long gone before anyone caught them. I doubt they did it to somebody local like Jackie. I was in the clear and thanked my boss and her husband for his help.

"Please thank your husband for whatever he did to get me out of this mess, please. Without him, I'd be in a lot of trouble right now, probably on my way back home or worse."

"It's disgraceful the way they treated you and others who were in your position. Never mind, they are found out now and will have to pay for what they did to these foreign workers."

My boss was really getting quite worked up about it all.

After that day, I never thought about it again. I just thanked God I had someone in power to help me. I never did find out what her husband did for a living, but he truly got them off my back, and I was never charged a cent. I also have no idea what happened to PD Bureau. Looking back, I suppose the right thing to do would've been to call Jackie and see if they were doing it to her as well. I hadn't even spoken to her since the guy with the van incident, and I doubted I ever would. I just guessed that our friendship had come to an end. No big loss if that's how she felt about me.

John started meeting me after work. He would wait down the street for me to finish work, and we would usually walk around, trying to find somewhere to eat dinner. I had gotten really close to him. Looking back, I suppose I was just very lonely. Everyone else had someone they lived with/screwed and I was all by myself. I know I lived with a family, but they had their own lives to live. I was sick of being all alone, and it seemed London kept throwing problems at me. It was nice to have someone to share stuff with who wasn't as old as my mom.

He would stay over sometimes at Miriam's. We still had to sleep in that single bed. There was a double one in the room next door to mine, but Miriam said it was Roy's bed (Roy was her son) and we couldn't use it. All the time I stayed at Miriam's house, I never saw Roy once and that double bed stayed unused. I should have pushed it.

There was something about two adults sleeping in a single bed. It was a very intimate thing to do. You had to be close—no moving to the other side of the bed as there *was* no other side of the bed. Maybe this had something to do with how close I felt to John. We did start out as friends, even though I didn't approve of his treatment of his former girlfriend. I must say though, you really had to get used to sleeping in rhythm, or it could get real uncomfortable real fast. Luckily, we were both small and thin. Couldn't imagine two fatter people in that tiny bed. That would never happen.

As it was, Miriam had some kind of mental problem and took to her bed. I mean, she took to her bed. We never saw or spoke to her. She never came out of that room except when she really needed to. Once or twice, I would see the girls bring her some food, but that was about it.

Once, she was in the kitchen with some pot and asked John to roll her a joint. He did it, but I was very uneasy watching him as he knew my opinion on smoking pot (or using any of the other drugs that all my friends had found). Miriam took the joint and went back to her room to smoke it. I guess it helped her to relax and get high. If she would've smoked it in the kitchen, I would have just left.

John was still living with Tacus, and the Aussie John and had gone back there for a few days. I didn't really trust him at all, so I called there. He had been acting strangely for a while, and I needed to know what was going on with him. Well, I found out. He came to the phone and could hardly speak. He sounded as if he were half asleep.

"You've been smoking pot with the guys, haven't you!?" I screamed at him.

I just got garbled words back, so I slammed down the phone.

I had broken up with a boyfriend in high school because of his pot smoking, and I sure wasn't going through that again with some guy I didn't know all that well and didn't really like all that much. I can't have a boyfriend who smokes pot or does drugs of any kind. So that would be the end of John—he obviously didn't care about what I thought and wanted to show off to his mates how cool he was. He could do whatever he wanted from now on. Good riddance. Thank God I didn't sleep with him—I mean have sex—I did sleep with him.

Chapter Ten

THE WEATHER WAS NOW GETTING a lot warmer in London with hardly any rain. According to locals, this was to be a really nice summer. I, for one, certainly hoped that was the case. This was certainly one place where dry and warm weather was appreciated, especially by me. You have to remember that the local Londoners were used to damp and dreary weather—they had grown up with it, and their bodies had adjusted. I had been thrust into living in wet conditions and without heat all at once, so I really did appreciate nice weather.

A while back, I had joined an agency to become an "au pair" girl in Paris. I figured I could keep up my French I learned in high school, see Paris, and get paid for the privilege. The whole situation really appealed to me. Of course, I never thought the whole thing through properly. I could get a weird family with horrible kids. My French could prove to be too inadequate to converse with Parisiens. But I did love the French language, and I was glad we had learned the Parisian kind in school.

So, breaking up with John proved to be just what I needed. I didn't really have anyone who really cared if I lived or died here. Lynn was still with Dennis, and they had both taken up smoking pot as well. Where they all got the money from, I'll never know.

Tacus, by the way, was a superb cook. A lot of Greek men are. I didn't really appreciate his cooking back then. He was one of the three who talked John into smoking pot, saying he would get "high." The Aussie John was still living with them, but I didn't pay any attention to him. I couldn't stand him nor he I. He was a terrible person, but everyone made excuses for him as he had been a medic in the Vietnam war for the Aussies. Good excuse to get high and act like a pompous jackass all the time.

I never saw Andy or Pete again after I left Fortescue House. I think someone told me Pete went back to Hull. Andy probably just found a new place until he finished his education. I think his parents had money, so he could afford to live somewhere a bit posher than Fortescue House, even though I think he liked it there. Maybe now I wasn't around to bring him his cup of tea in the morning, he had no reason to stay. HA!!!

I would miss my job, and of course, the ladies who had been so kind to me. I would also miss my city—I loved London so much. But I had come over here to see some places in Europe, not just London. I hadn't intended on being stuck in one place for the rest of my stay. And of course, Paris was a lot closer to Luxembourg for my return flight to Toronto. I was getting quite excited about the move and was looking forward to it.

Guess what? Well, you've seen my luck with things happening to me in London throughout this book, haven't you? I got a letter in the mail from the Paris "au pair" people. They wanted A LOT of money for setting me up with a family in Paris. The letter sounded really dodgey to me, and it was very contradictory to what I had been told would happen and what the costs involved would be. I plain couldn't afford to take them up on their offer. I didn't have enough money and sure wasn't going to spend all of what I did have on a fishy sounding adventure. It wasn't just the money, the whole letter sounded off, and I resigned myself to not going to Paris and staying in a city I loved and in a job I loved. I have NEVER regretted that decision. It was the right one for me at the time.

I lived in a huge city with plenty to do. In 1970, the population of London was 8,594,000. The population of my whole country was 21,374,326. This meant that one third of the population of my whole country lived in Greater London. That's a lot of people and a lot of sights to see. So, instead of just walking about to nowhere in particular, I started looking at touristy things.

I bought myself a camera—remember mine was destroyed by my stealing butter in Luxembourg. I thought I'd like some snaps of this great town to take home. It felt strange taking snaps of sights I saw all the time just because I was supposed to as a tourist. I surely didn't feel like one and hoped I didn't act like one. Except of course while I was taking photos of places like Trafalgar Square, Buckingham Palace, Big Ben, Westminster Abbey and Parliament. My two favourites were Tower Bridge and the Tower of London. What amazing sights they both were. I didn't know the history behind the tower. I didn't actually go in it; I just took pics. I was a passive tourist. It was just plain laziness on my part not to study these places while I had them on my doorstep. Classrooms of students went to the tower to actually see where history was made and not just read about it.

Then something surprising happened. John had been calling Miriam's a lot to try to talk to me, but I wouldn't talk to him. As a result, he started showing up on the street below where I worked, waiting for me to finish for the day. He worked nights for London Transport. It was awkward because I really didn't want to see him. I'd seen too much of his horrible side and had avoided him for a long while.

"Why don't you just go and see what he wants, dear?" one of my ladies asked me.

"Don't really want to. I've broken up with him."

"Seems he doesn't know that."

My guess was they wanted to know what he wanted as well. Probably, they were all sick of his hanging around. So, after a bit, I went to see what he wanted.

"We'll be here if you run into any trouble. Just wave to us and we'll come down."

What lovely women they all were.

"What is it you want with me!?" I yelled at him.

"I just want to talk to you. I'm sorry I smoked pot when I know how you feel about it."

"You were just so sneaky about it. Pretending to just go out with the boys. You know what I think about drugs, and I'm not interested in anyone who does them. Certainly not as a boyfriend. I don't even like you very much. You treated Barbara like shit. I'd love to punch you for her."

"I deserve anything you want to throw at me, but I really like you, and I am sorry I upset you so much."

"I can't be bothered with anyone who can so easily be talked into doing the wrong thing. You didn't even get high from the pot, you only got sleepy."

"Let me explain. I was just sucked into what they wanted me to do. I'm not like you, I have trouble saying no to people."

"Just to macho mates who you don't want to loose face with. You have no trouble treating women like shit. I'm not going to be treated like that by you."

"I don't expect you to."

"Oh yes, you do. But that's not going to happen. I'd rather be on my own than take any crap from a guy. I'm quite happy here on my own. I've been having fun."

I told him about my recent weekend travels around the city and the interesting places London had to offer for those not going to the pub all the time. I had grown to appreciate some of what this lovely city had to offer its residences (me being one of them) if they were willing to look.

That's where I made my mistake, by talking normally to him. That's all he needed.

"Let's go for a walk and talk about things. We used to get along really well before the pot thing."

"Not really. You only asked me out because that blond broad you were interested in at the pub told you to get stuffed."

"That's not true."

"I was there, remember?"

"Let's not fight. Can we walk some place and try to find some food for dinner?"

What a mistake that was. Before I knew it, he was back sleeping—sleeping, mind you—in my small single bed. Not with me very much because he worked nights and I worked days, so I pretty well had the bed to myself at night.

How had this happened? I didn't really know except John was really good at getting what he wanted from people, not just women (although he was good at that too).

I'll tell you one thing that happened when I first met John at Fortescue House. This may explain his need to fit in or whatever his need was. At that time, he sported a mustache and two sideburns. Both looked ridiculous to me, but I especially hated the 'tash. It didn't suit him, and I told him so. Next time I saw him, it was gone. He'd shaved it off. He still had his sideburns, but the 'tash was gone. He looked much better, and I told him so.

"But Barbara really liked it," he revealed to me.

"So why did you shave it off?"

"Don't really know why I did that."

That's John in a nut shell. He cared what other people thought about him while I'd stopped doing that a long time ago. I found it gets you nowhere trying to please everybody else, so you'd better please yourself. Isn't that a song? It's yourself who you end up living with in the real world, and it doesn't really matter what anyone seems to think about what you do or don't do. But I guess everyone is different, and John did care what people's opinions were, especially their opinions about him. Anyway, it got rid of the stupid mustache.

I was having a reoccurring dream/nightmare. If someone cared to analyze it, I'm sure it would mean something very scary. I was at work and walking down the long, long set of stairs they had there. I was carrying a large tray with all our tea things on it (still hot and unused). I tripped, and me, the tray, and the hot tea things went tumbling down the stairs. I had this dream so often, I really didn't know if it had actually happened or not.

Work was going great. I really enjoyed the work and interacting with mostly upper crust, posh people. I say that, and you may wonder what I mean. The agency delt with high-end jobs, so that's who I delt with. As an outsider, I could really see the class thing up close. It was and is a real thing. I wish I had more examples to give—it was just an accepted reality to observe.

I'm sure nobody thought they were all alcoholics either but a lot were. The few who didn't drink, often didn't because of their health being compromised from years of over drinking. Pub hours then were restrictive. Weekdays were from 10:30 a.m. to 2 p.m. OR 11 a.m. to 3 p.m. and then 5:30 p.m. to 10:30 p.m. (sometimes until 11 p.m.). On Sunday, they didn't open until 12 p.m. to 2 p.m. and then 7 p.m. to 10:30 p.m. Also, back then, not many guys drove, so that was something. At least not the guys I knew, who had no money to run a car. Even if they did drive, there was no such thing as any thought toward drunk driving. They just drove when they wanted to, drunk or not.

I did like the English people. As a whole, they were very polite. An often asked question was/is "Are you alright?" They were very formal as well, especially in their dress. The older men in the pub would often wear suits and a tie for God's sake. This was normal wear for them. John told me he had a "drinking suit" while at home in Hull. He wasn't kidding.

It always seemed to me that everyone was into some sort of a fiddle to get something for nothing type of thing. I found their work ethic to be lacking. Hence my being hired by my permanent employer. Nor were they good at cleaning. You could see examples of it all over the place from washrooms (toilets in particular) to the state of the rooms we rented. I'd hate to guess when any of those mattresses/sheets/blankets had been changed or even washed. I had real problems with their lifestyle. The drinking, screwing around, and now pot smoking. Take John and Pete, for example. When Lynn and I moved into Fortescue House, we had seen a lot, and I mean a lot, of London in the short time we'd been in London. The two guys next door had seen the nearest pub. Mind you, the only people I knew were struggling students or poor workers who lived in bed sits. My salvation was in my work ladies.

Or so I thought. They often left for lunch (they got luncheon vouchers too) and often had a few drinks (I could smell it on them) before coming back to work. One afternoon, one of my favourite co-workers came back to work from lunch drunk as anything. She couldn't walk straight.

"Her husband took her out for her lunch, and she hadn't seen him in a while," someone told me.

I believe he was some big shot who worked away from home a lot.

"I'm going to take her home."

"Good idea, before the boss sees her," I replied.

I doubted the boss would even care much. They were very laid-back there. If ever I were late, I got "never mind" or "it doesn't matter." Not that I was late very much.

Public transportation in London was very, very reliable once you got the hang of it. The tube map posted on all the stations was really easy to read and follow, but you had to be very careful. These stations were as far down as you could go into the earth sometimes, and you walked and walked and walked a long way to even catch a train. Often, you would have to change a few times as well. Sometimes, it was way faster to either walk or take the bus. Of course, taking the bus offered views you didn't get on the tube. On the other hand, if you were in a hurry (like getting to work on time), the tube was the only way to go.

It was the age of the miniskirt, but this was a very conservative firm. Women couldn't even wear a pant suit to work in and must wear tights under their dresses. This was something I wasn't used to doing. Of course, the women I worked with wouldn't wear minis. They were all my mother's age or older and very prim and proper, except for the odd drunken lunch. I had always worn minis, but now I wore them with tights on. I was very thin and small enough to get away with it. Kind of like a poor version of Twiggy.

I hadn't really done much sightseeing, even though I'd spent a few weekends taking some photos and looking around by myself. Now that John was in the picture, so to speak, my weekends weren't my own anymore. We didn't really sightsee in our spare time. I suppose meeting me after work and walking around before coming home was sightseeing as we saw plenty of sights, but to us, they were just there, if you know what I mean. On weekends, I think we were just getting to know each other, and so we stayed home or travelled around Denmark Hill and Camberwell Green. Usually, I was tired or needed to go shopping. It was kind of like a person living in Toronto and never going up the CN Tower. Many attractions went on throughout the week while I was working, i.e. the changing of the guards at Buckingham Palace, so I had no chance to see them.

I hadn't heard from Jackie, and I kind of decided to forget about her as a girlfriend of mine. We were so different, her and

I, but it wasn't that I didn't like her, I did. She and her family had been very good to me the whole time I'd been there. We just had very different ideas of what was fun. I thought she'd call if she wanted something from me. Most probably, she was waiting until I went home. I did miss her company; she was fun in her own way. More importantly, I also missed going to her local pub with her and seeing everyone. Maybe we'd get together to say goodbye before I left to go home. Who knew what was to come? I sure didn't—not in this exciting city.

Chapter Eleven

WELL . . . SOMEHOW JOHN MOVED IN with me. I don't really know how that happened. I suppose he was spending so much time there, mostly sleeping, that it was crazy for him to pay rent for the place with John and Tacus. God, if anyone (my mom) back home knew I was living with a guy, I didn't know what they'd say. It just wasn't done in 1970, even in England with their lack of morals. Lynn seemed to be the exception.

We didn't really see a lot of each other. I worked all day, and he worked all night. Sometimes, he'd be home to sleep a while before I left for work. He would still meet me after work, and we'd hang out for a little before he went to work. He still worked for London Transport, not very far from where we lived, so he took me home before getting ready for work himself.

I was pretty lonely, really. Sounds so exciting, doesn't it? Being nineteen and living with a guy. I might as well have been by myself.

Then as usual, something happened to liven up my little life. We got bed bugs in that tiny little single bed. It makes me sick to this day when I think about them. There was some kind of a shop downstairs that sold food, so I imagine that's where the bugs came from. I didn't know what they were at first, but John sure did.

"What a buggy country this is. First, we all got head lice, and now it's bed bugs." I was so disgusted.

So, while he worked night shift, I slept on the chair. It never occurred to me it may have bugs in it as well, so that's where I slept, dreaming of bugs climbing all over me. It took a good week before Miriam had the place fumigated. I remember John had to take the bed apart, and we had to leave for the day.

We only had weekends to do everything other than work. One Friday night after work, John told me he was going to see strippers tomorrow with his friend Danny. Danny was a work friend of his who also had a job selling newspapers at Oxford Street tube station.

"Really?" came my answer. *Just another pervert, just like my Dad,* I thought to myself. "Off you go then."

And the next day, he did.

I decided two could play this stupid game, called Jackie and arranged to meet her at the pub that night. John knew all about the guy with the van, and the drive home from this pub. I didn't tell him I was going; I just went. And I had a really good time. While at the pub, Jackie and I talked about the guy and the van incident. I don't know if she believed me about what actually happened. I think she was just mad it wasn't her that he took home. Anyway, we cleared the air and sort of became friends again.

Sunday morning was a riot.

"Where were you last night?"

"Thought I'd go see some strippers myself."

"Don't be so stupid."

"Stupid? You should talk. You started all this with your friends, smoking pot, seeing strippers, and I don't like it. I've told you all this before. If this is what you want to do, you're with the wrong girl. I'm not being treated like I'm not around.

I'm not Barbara. I think we'd better forget all this again. I've had enough bullshit to last a lifetime. I can do whatever I want to, and if you're going to leave me alone, that's exactly what I'm going to do."

"I didn't think going out with Danny would cause all this hassel. I wouldn't have bothered."

"I know you're used to doing whatever you want whenever you want, but I'm not putting up with it. I'm not with you to be by myself all the time. We hardly see each other as it is. If that's OK by you, I want you to move out."

He just turned and left. I guess no girl had ever told him what he could or couldn't do before, and he didn't know how to handle it. I didn't care. Nobody was treating me like this!

Thank God I didn't have sex with him. What a complication it would have been. Not for him, he'd just move on to his next conquest. *I'm better off without him*, I thought. Although I didn't really think so somehow. I didn't love him, but he had something, a way of getting his own way, I suppose, and I would miss being with him.

I didn't have to wait very long to see him again. A bit later, he came back. He obviously had a front door key from working the night shift. I was still sitting on the bed where I was when he had left. I really didn't know what to expect from him, but I knew I wasn't going to back down.

"What if I promise never to smoke pot again?"

"That would be a start. But what about leaving me on my own when you go to the pub or wherever you go. I know that's what guys do here, but I can't live like that long term. I realize you went to see strippers to impress Danny, but I need you to impress me not him." I was not a happy lady. "I'm not going to stay at home night after night while you go out by yourself. I see it at the pub all the time. Most of those guys hitting on me are married with kids at home."

"I'm sorry I went to see strippers with Danny. It was a joke, really. Just some old lady half undressing. It was pretty sad to watch."

"You didn't know that when you set off. She could've been gorgeous with big boobs as well—you didn't know."

"Anyway, I'm sorry."

"I don't need you to be sorry. I need you to do stuff that you don't have to say sorry for doing. I won't be treated like my mom was, so I really think you've got the wrong girlfriend. God! I won't even sleep with you."

"We sleep together all the time."

"Sex, stupid. I mean sex. I can't deal with all this macho crap. The guys back home aren't like this. I have tons of friends who are guys, and they have more time for me than you ever did or do now. This may be normal for English girls to handle, they grow up with it, but I won't stand for it. You know me. This is not the first time we've had this same conversation. You are promising not to smoke pot again only because you didn't get high from it, only sleepy, so it's no big deal for you to give it up."

"OK. I won't leave you alone so much as well. What do you think? I can only try to be more considerate. I've never had to do that with anyone else before. I really like you and want to stay here."

You have to remember, all these conversations took place over fifty-one years ago, so the words aren't exact, but the message sure is. I didn't know what to expect from him. Could he change so he could be with me? Did I want him to change? I didn't want his personality to change, that's what I liked about him, but his bad behaviour had to. I didn't think it was too much to ask for the guy you live with to pay attention to you. Was it? But, could I trust he'd keep his word? I didn't know that much about him, except that he had treated his last girlfriend very badly. Just because that's the way most Englishmen treated women didn't mean he had the right to treat me that way. I needed time to really think about what I wanted out of this situation.

"I need some time by myself to work all this out. I don't know if I can put up with your crap or if I can meet you somewhere in the middle. But I do know I need you to be gone. Go and stay with Tacus and John for a while and don't contact me until I'm ready. I'll let you know when."

"If that's what you want, OK."

And he left once more.

I didn't have anyone to talk to about this. I certainly didn't want to be told I should stay with him and put up with his crap. I didn't feel right talking to Lynn; we wouldn't have much to say to each other as we weren't that close. The ladies at work wouldn't want to be involved that much in my personal life.

It must have been May by now, and the weather as predicted was quite nice (for England). I tried to put John to the back of my mind and get on with my work and my life. Somehow, he always crept into my thoughts. I don't really know why. I suppose I was attracted to him, and we did have some fun together at times. I was awfully lonely at night, and I was sick of being on my own. About a week or so after he left, I went around to see him. He had been good and didn't call or bother me at work during that time (which must have taken some doing on his part).

"I'd like you to move back in but on my terms."

This was very hard for me and VERY unlike what I would normally do. Don't ask me why this was happening. I didn't know then, and I still don't know today. He had something I wanted. Don't know what.

His immediate answer was, "I'll come right now."

He started collecting all the rest of his things from around the flat.

We were alone in the flat. His two roomates were out, thank God. I wouldn't want to do this in front of them. I was praying I wasn't making the biggest mistake of my life doing this, but I had made up what was left of my tiny little mind. I'd rather put up with some garbage than be without him. Why? Dunno, dunno why. Was I going to be one of those women who settled? I sure hoped not.

So, we were back at Miriam's together, living together, sleeping together, but that's about all. We engaged in lots of sexual activity, just not penetration. To me, sex went with marriage, and of course, could lead to pregnancy, especially in someone as stupid about sex as I was. It was increasingly obvious that this wasn't going to be enough for John. He was used to screwing his girlfriends, even if it were only once a week in the back of a Mini. My morals didn't matter.

Apart from sexual attention, I didn't get much else from John. I wasn't really in his life apart from that. A throwback from his upbringing I suppose. Shouldn't I have wanted to have sex with him? I guess so, but I didn't really. I had this idea that I needed to be married first. All my life, I'd heard about my mom and my many aunts who all HAD to get married because they were all knocked up. What a reason to marry someone. I was determined for that not to happen to me.

You have to remember, I'd not done much in the way of sex. Maybe some petting and kissing but nothing like what I did with John. I went to work at this posh place with hickeys all over my neck. "Love bites" John called them. They just looked terrible to me, and I was embarrassed a lot. My women knew exactly what I'd been up to.

One time, when we were hot and heavy doing everything but penetration, he decided it was time for his dick to be used.

"What do you think you're doing?"

"Let's have proper sex."

"No, I don't want to."

The penis was still in place.

"This is called rape. Stop right now."

And he did.

We never spoke about this incident after it happened. I suppose he was very frustrated doing everything but penetration and thought he'd push it. I'm not making excuses for him because if he had gone through with it, it most certainly would have been rape.

Now what is that called when a man puts his finger(s) in your vagina and uses it like a penis? Oh yes—finger fucking. We did a lot of that, and I suppose John didn't see any difference between a finger and a penis. With a finger, I was still a virgin and could never ever get pregnant.

What a shame neither one of us knew there was/is a small organ that gives a lot of pleasure to a woman called a clitoris. Why is it no one bothers to learn anything about sex before they actually do it? I suppose men assume they know what they're doing (maybe through other men's tales and exaggerations, or through porn) so they can't be bothered to learn anything else. Most girls back then knew nothing either, so that didn't help. You certainly weren't in a position to criticize what was being done to you because you didn't know any better. So, as a woman, you ended up with crappy sex. Only, you didn't know it was crappy sex because it's the only kind you ever got.

John began saying a phrase often, "I think we should indulge," meaning, of course, have sex. I knew this was going to happen whether I wanted to or not. After all, I went and got him to move back in with me, didn't I? Seriously, what did I think was going to happen? We were living together. So, it was down to me again. Have sex or lose John, simple as that. How many times have you heard that one? Especially being applied to teenagers. Oh look—I was a teenager. To me, virginity was the one thing that stopped girls from being slutty. Once it was gone, well, it was gone, and there was nothing there then to stop you from having sex with the next guy and so on.

I found it strange that males were just "blokes getting some" if they slept around, but females were sluts if they did the same thing. Who were these girls the guys were sleeping with? What a double standard! To date, nothing has changed in this regard.

I knew John had condoms, and I wasn't quite sure about the birth control pill. It was pretty new, and I didn't know a lot about it. He was used to having safe sex, so I suppose I had to trust him and pray I wouldn't get pregnant. To have sex with this man, I was going against my morals and what I believed in. He was twenty-three and I was nineteen. He'd slept with his fair share of broads, and of course, he knew I was a virgin. God, I was going to be just like everyone else.

We agreed on a night to do this. I don't know what I expected. Oh yes, I do. I expected romance, an out-of-body experience, the pure passion that you read in books about someone losing their virginity. Boy, that wasn't what I got. There was no foreplay, no kissing, nothing at all like that. He just stuck his dick in hard and it really hurt. There was quite a lot of blood all over my landlady's sheets as well. Guess that meant I was no longer a virgin. It had to be one of the worst things that has ever happened to me.

"Do you know what to do after you've had a bit?" John asked of me as if we had just a really good time.

"Not really. Guess I'll clean up the blood." I hurt too much to get up right at that moment, so I just lay there.

"I'll be late for work."

And off he went on the night shift. I'd like to think he was ashamed of what he just did, but I really doubted it. He just didn't want to stay around to see what he'd just done.

I knew Barbara had been a virgin. He probably did the same thing to her in the back of her Mini. Why did I know all these things about his sex life? He told me, of course. He used to brag about the number of women he'd screwed—trying to impress me, I suppose. All it did was the opposite. *Another jerk screwing around,* I thought to myself. They call it getting experience, but doing the same things to different girls isn't experience. It's just a guy bragging about what a stud he is to me, and I suppose, to his friends. I don't know if men talk about their conquests or not to other men, but they sure do to their women. I couldn't get a number out of him though. Of course, the implication was that there were millions. The truth was something else, but he didn't think I deserved to be told this number. Even when faced with the fact that he brought all this up, not me, I didn't get an answer. *Sod him,* I thought. This was great for him as he knew he was the only person I had slept with.

I knew, of course, that this was just "breaking me in" or whatever men call it. I sure hoped sex would be good or even OK. Just because he slept with others didn't mean he knew what he was doing or how to make ME feel good. *Guess I'll find out,* I thought.

I gave up much more than my virginity that night. I gave up some of me, and I wasn't happy. To be fair, when we were doing sexual things, my vagina got really wet, and I sometimes felt like having sex. Maybe this was the only bad part.

It was. We didn't have proper sex for a while because I was still very sore. For me, it wasn't much different than what we'd already been doing, except now a great ruddy penis was thrusting into my vagina instead of a finger. A great ruddy penis that was very capable of getting me pregnant. After my brother's trouble, that was all my mom needed—my coming home with a big belly. A condom was always used, and I had to trust John that he did it properly. How had I gotten into this position? Never before in my life had I relied on someone else to not screw up. I always did exactly what I wanted up until now. It was my decision to give in, and I was stuck with it. *Will I turn into a slut after I'm finished with John???* I sort of felt like I betrayed myself and what I believed in. After John's treatment of Barbara,

I had no reason to believe he would treat me any differently. Especially since I would be going home in a few months.

Since lives don't revolve solely around sex, we did do other things. After all, we lived in this great city. I had seen a lot more of it than John, so we started to sightsee a bit more. We felt like such tourists, but that's exactly what we were. We certainly were never going to be "Londoners" even if we lived the rest of our lives in this lovely big town.

We really only had weekends to see the sights as I still worked five days a week and John worked night shift at Lambeth North tube station (where the Imperial War Museum is). He installed some wrought iron stairs there. So as long as he worked for London Transport, and I travelled with him, my travel was free. He just showed his pass, and the conductor waved his hand to say OK mate. That's how crooked they all were. So that made seeing London sights pretty cheap. Most of the museums were free to get into, and mostly the transport was free. The tube didn't go out as far as Denmark Hill, so we usually took buses.

Miriam was still depressed and held up in her bedroom. We never saw her, and we really didn't know what to do, so we did nothing. Both of her daughters seemed to have disappeared, and we didn't know why or where to. So really, we had the whole house to ourselves—to watch TV, use the kitchen, and more importantly, have a shared bath. Since the bath was in the kitchen, it was really weird to be naked with a guy, in a bath, in a kitchen. There was a hatch between the living room and the kitchen, so anyone could see us, although, why anyone would bother is beyond me.

The water there and most of England was very hard, so by the time the bath was over, there was this scum rolling over the top of the water. You, of course, had to wash and rinse your hair in this water. No such thing as a shower then.

Spring turned into summer, and as predicted, it was warm and mostly sunny. I even stopped putting a hot water bottle in my bed at night for the first time since I arrived in this city. London in the warmth without rain was a joy to walk around in. People weren't as miserable. It made me fall more in love with the place.

I got to know the person I was having sex with a lot better and started to like him more than I used to. I understood more about what his upbringing had been like. His family were quite poor (living in Hull), and his dad sounded like a great guy. His mom had died just before I met him, and he never talked about her. His dad remarried a woman he'd been friends with, so John had a stepmother.

John often talked about "serving his time." I thought he'd been in jail and was afraid to ask what for. That's how much I wanted to be with him. It turns out that's an English expression for serving your apprenticeship in his work field (being a millwright).

We hadn't seen Lynn and Dennis in a while, so we went to Fortescue House. We didn't stay long because they were moving the next day. Finally, after living off Lynn for months and months, Dennis actually got a job as a bike delivery guy. He bought a motorcycle, so I guessed that was how he got the job.

"You'll have to come see us at our new place," Lynn told me and gave me their new address. "When did you start living with John? I thought you didn't like him very much."

"Oh, a while now. He sort of grew on me. I guess I've been lonely. You never come to see me." Not once had Lynn been to Miriam's.

"I know. Now that Dennis works, he likes to smoke pot on the weekends, and you don't like that, so we don't come over."

"I remember when Dennis told me he could take pot if it came his way, but he wasn't bothered. That's the trouble with drugs of any kind, even booze. You think you can handle it until you can't.

"No more lectures, please."

"OK. But come see us some time. We live in southeast London, and it's nice there. Anyway, you have to pack. Good luck with the move, and we'll keep in touch."

Whether we would or not remained to be seen. All the time we had lived in London, Lynn had never once asked about how I was or made any kind of an effort to contact me to see if I were alive or dead. But should she have a problem, there I was to help. Some friendship that was.

John and I had broken the pattern of going to the pub every night. Kind of hard to do while you work at night. I'm quite sure he had a few pints on the way to pick me up from work. But to be fair, I didn't find John to be a typical English drinker. He seemed to be able to either take it or leave it alone when required. Not many could do that. For most of them, it was a pint after work or die trying. Trouble was, most stayed at the pub too long before going home to their families, and that's what I objected to, not the actual drinking as such. Don't get me wrong. I liked going to the pub. It was a very social place to meet with your friends and have a drink, but I had seen the other side of it. It was just something they all did and would continue to do despite my condescending opinions. Right?

One afternoon, we were walking across a zebra crossing (can't remember exactly where) when a bloke shoved John as he walked by us.

"Watch it, mate," he said to John.

Turns out he was a skinhead. These were guys who shaved their heads, wore suspenders and Dr. Martens boots. They loved to pick fights and beat the shit out of people. I guess today was our turn. They were bullies who travelled in packs. I would've guessed there were four or five of them and the two of us. That seemed to be the odds they liked.

Well, before any of them could do anything, John smacked one of them over the head with Miriam's umbrella and another was struck in the belly. It was incredible. One of John's hobbies was fencing, and the moves sure came in handy for this fight, I'll tell you. One guy ended up falling against a paper box. The rest just ran away before they got beaten up as well. It was just like in an action movie where, of course, there is always just one jock against a lot of others ready to beat him to a pulp. But this was real life.

I was impressed with this guy. Mind you, growing up, John had to learn to defend himself as he was rather short and had a great big chip on his shoulder to go with it. All I know is he saved himself from a beating. God knows what they would've done to me. I didn't want to think about it. Of course, no one who was around to help him in any way. Needless to say, he wrecked Miriam's umbrella, and we threw it in the bin. Maybe he wasn't so bad after all. Just as well, as I was living with him and having sex with him. I still shutter to think what the other outcome could have been. I probably wouldn't be writing this now.

Chapter Twelve

LIVING WITH JOHN GOT VERY comfortable. We mostly got along great. He stopped working nights and got a day job— still with London Transport, just a day job. We were spending a lot more time together now, and I started to like him a lot more. I still didn't take any shit, and if any came my way, I soon got rid of it. It didn't happen very often. I think he knew what would happen if he pushed me too far. What I didn't understand was why HE put up with the way I was. He sure wasn't used to being with someone who didn't do what she was told. Maybe he realized that's who I was, and I wasn't going to change for anyone. Maybe I amused him, who knew? Maybe he was just sick of trying to pick up unknown broads in the pub for a quick shag, who knew? Not me.

I found sex very frustrating. I didn't know I was supposed to have something called an orgasm, and I certainly didn't have any. He did because that meant the end of sex after banging away quite happily until he came. I got quite a lot of foreplay because we were used to doing that before penetration entered (so to speak) the picture. I quite enjoyed that part, but the actual fucking part wasn't that interesting to me. I could imagine some poor teenage girl letting some guy do this to "prove she loved him," getting nothing out of it, and maybe getting pregnant for her stupidity. Was I any different? NOPE!!!! Maybe that was part of why I didn't enjoy the sex much. As well as the fear of getting pregnant and going home with a big belly, there was always my mind that I was doing something wrong.

Even though John had slept with numerous women, it sure didn't mean he knew what he was doing. How does doing the same thing to a lot of different people make you experienced? Like I said before, why not find out what to do? Experiment? Not for John. I couldn't even touch his balls nor his neck. I tried to have sex getting on top, and that seemed to work a bit better. A least I got something out of it. I suppose I was rubbing my clitoris to get some action without knowing it. I liked going on top because I could control how far his dick went in. Apparently, the feeling is at the opening, so I was doing what I could to get off—never worked—again, there was no clit action.

I guess the sex was pretty good for John. Better I'd guess than in the back of a Mini which was what he was used to doing with Barbara. Wonder where they parked the car in London?

Something very odd happened one morning. We were in Miriam's kitchen making a cup of tea when he started rambling away.

"What if you didn't have to go home? What if you stayed here, and we lived in the same country?"

He wasn't making any sense.

"I do have to go home. My stay is only for one year. That's all I can stay in England."

"I know, but what if we could stay together longer?"

"How?"

"We could think of a way, couldn't we?"

What was this guy on about? I HAD to leave here by the end of September, or they'd throw me out. I really didn't know what to make of all of this. Then, it hit me.

"Are you asking me to marry you?"

"I guess I am, yes."

"You want to marry me? Why?"

"I think we'd make a good team. You can carry your weight and more, unlike the women in this country."

No mention of love. How did I feel about this? Not good. My mother loved my father and look where it got her.

"We'd make a good team? What are we, a football team? What does that mean? Just a few months ago, you asked Barbara to marry you. Look at how that turned out. You're a very fickle person. I don't think you know what you want."

"I think I love you and want to stay with you when you go home. I've always wanted to immigrate. I nearly went to Aussie a few years back when they had a ten quid deal going."

"So, you want to come to Canada with me? Why get married? You could just immigrate—it doesn't have to be with me."

"I want to be with you though."

So, we bought a ring. It was a diamond solitaire and cost £50 which was a hell of a lot of money for us (note I say us). I wanted to pick out my own ring. I could never understand men who go ahead and buy a ring hoping that the girl might like it. What if she doesn't? Should she tell him he has lousy taste or wear a ring she hates for the rest of her life?

We had a lot to work out, money to save, and plans to make. John always thought everything would work out fine, so most of the planning was left up to me.

The first thing was to find out about my ticket home from Luxembourg. It wasn't refundable as I had thought, so unless we both wanted to travel there (which upon reflection, might have been a nice trip) that ticket was useless to me. So, we needed two tickets from Heathrow to Toronto at around £100 per ticket. Cheap one-way fares didn't exist in 1970. I had my money, but I doubted John did. Mind you, if this was his plan all along, maybe he had been saving all along. Who knew? Not me. Apparently, he did have some saved, but of course, not quite enough. However, we still had time. It was only June, so he had a few months to save.

Was all this pushing for sex and living together leading up to this? I suppose it was. Did he really love me or was this just a way to come to Canada? And to a ready-made family and a free place to live (my mom's). I shut all that out of my mind. I was engaged to be married. I sometimes would look at my ring to reassure myself that I was doing nothing wrong while I had sex. A lot of my friends thought the same way I did, so I didn't (and don't) think I was strange. What was strange to me was the casual way everyone bonked everyone else just because they could. Talk about casual sex!!

My ladies at work would often say to me, "Don't be in such a hurry to get married, dear. It's not all it's cracked up to be, believe me."

As well, I knew a lot from my mom and dad's so-called marriage. But I would be different. Right?

Since John was immigrating, and not simply coming to Canada for a holiday, he had to go through the process so he could stay, live and work there. I left him to it.

"I can't do anything to help you. You'll have to do it on your own."

"I know. I hate this kind of stuff, but I have to get it done by myself. You can't help."

Not that I would. This was his baby, not mine.

And he did, of course, or there would be no immigration. He actually figured it out (with the help of immigration people, who I assumed, knowing John, did most of it for him). This must have been something he really wanted. Funny enough, he had to deal with Canada House, so that was very convenient for him (after I showed him where it was, as he had no idea). I think he did all of this between jobs during the day because they would've been closed after work. Another fiddle.

So, the plans were flying along. The legal part was nearly done, his saving for a ticket was well in hand, and he seemed pleased to be doing it all. I supposed he thought he would be heading to a better life. I, of course, had written everyone saying I was engaged and that I was bringing him home to live in Canada. There was never a question of my living in his country. While I loved London, it was as an outsider. I couldn't take the cold, damp, dreary weather, nor the drinking problems, or any other social problems I didn't like. I sure couldn't see myself bringing up kids there. I lived in the best country in the world, and I wanted John to see what he had been missing.

Money was fine (at least for me). Miriam didn't increase my rent when John moved in, so we both lived there and had use of the house for £4/week. I don't even remember if John paid his half. At Fortescue House, Lynn and I each paid £4 for a bed as did everyone else. Abdul made a killing there.

We started to see the city again on the weekends. After living here nearly a year, I couldn't go home without seeing the place properly. The Tower of London was magnificent. Just looking at it from afar was uplifting and took your breath away. Mine anyway. We, of course, were too cheap to pay for a tour to find out about the history, so we actually learned nothing, even though we went in which wasn't free either. We did a lot of walking. As I've said many times, London is a town for walking, especially in the nicer weather. The sights were all there to see and mostly all free.

One Saturday, we took the bus up to Stratford-upon-Avon. What a lovely little place. A lot nicer than the one in Ontario. We saw the house where Shakespeare was born and spent his childhood. We also saw Anne Hathaway's Cottage, which was outside of the town centre but well worth the walk. On the River Avon, there's the Royal Shakespeare Theatre. We didn't go in. It was an interesting old place, and I'm glad we went.

One lunchtime, I went to Shaftesbury Theatre and bought two tickets to see *Hair* the play. There was a lot of censorship trying to immerge as the play dealt with drugs and nudity, and I suppose was quite risky for 1970. We went to see it or tried to see it. I guess the ticket agent thought I was an American because he sold me terrible seats behind a column. We could hardly see anything. We both knew there was no sense in complaining.

We also saw Dudley Moore in *Play it Again, Sam.* I remember the ticket cost 10/6 because that was my hourly pay rate when I worked for PD Bureau.

The best play we saw, however, was called *Abelard and Heloise* which starred Diana Rigg of the *The Avengers* fame. I actually saw Mrs. Peel nude. I don't remember much about the play itself, but I do remember people saying that the nude bit was totally unnecessary. Not true. I still remember the play for it, don't I?

And so, our life went on—living, working, sightseeing—in London for the time we had left. I started taking more photos of famous landmarks to show the guys at home. We rarely saw anyone else, not Jackie, the guys from Fortescue House, nor Lynn and Dennis.

But as I was remaining in one place and had a permanent address, my friends and family started writing me, curious to find out what I was up to. It was nice to finally hear from home and to have someone to write to. I love writing letters to people, always have done. My mom only ever complained about the boys (my brothers). The two little ones were always in trouble, and of course, the oldest had knocked up his girlfriend. She was not a happy lady but still had her job, which probably kept her as sane as a mother with four boys could be. I think most were disappointed in things I did as I was doing much the same things they were, only in London.

We needed to decide when the flight one-way to Canada would happen because John wanted to say goodbye to his relatives both in Hull and in Scotland (where his father was born). We settled on mid-September and bought our tickets. John's passport had arrived the week before, so we were all set.

"I want to say goodbye to everyone. God only knows when I'll be back to see them again."

"Well, Vie's son Dave and his family live in Burlington, so maybe they'll come over to see them and us."

Vie was John's dad's new wife (his stepmother). No one liked her very much, but I did. We got along great. Maybe it was because I came from where her son now lived.

"That's true. I'm meant to be making all this money over there, so I guess we can come back as well."

He'd been told he would make a packet in Canada in his trade. The grass is always greener, isn't it?

I was looking forward to going home where there was heat in the toilets and bedrooms. Nobody walked around in the rain all day long. To be fair, if Londoners didn't walk in the rain, they'd never go out. Plus, I didn't fancy having a cold for the rest of my life.

If you think about it, it must have been a big deal for John. It would be a completely different life for him (although, he was being eased into it by living with me all this time). Mind you, he wouldn't be going to a strange place alone as I had done coming here. He wouldn't have to find a place to live as I had done. He'd be moving into my mom's place (as would I) with a ready-made family. He'd be marrying me. Also, he'd have a free place to stay until he found a job. I imagined the plane ticket and ring pretty well made him broke. He was assured by everyone that he'd have no trouble getting work in his field.

Chapter Thirteen

SUDDENLY AND WITHOUT WARNING, THE end of August appeared as if out of nowhere. I had given my notice at work when we bought our plane tickets to Canada, but it was still hard to say goodbye to my ladies. They had been so nice to me for the last six months while I was working with them. I really would miss them all. I wasn't so easily replaced as they soon found out. My replacement worked at an English pace like everyone else there. I would certainly miss my work and the posh area I worked in.

So, it was time to leave Miriam's. We had packed up all our stuff. I had considerably more clothing than when I moved in so had to buy another suitcase to carry it all in. John had all his records and record player as well as all his clothes. Some of the things couldn't come to Canada with us, and he was going to leave a lot with his sister in Hull.

Miriam actually got out of bed to say goodbye and to offer to call us a cab to the station. There was far too much to carry on the free bus. John still had his pass for some reason. I would certainly miss this place. We said our goodbyes, lying through our teeth by saying we would keep in touch. God, we weren't in touch when we lived in the same house together.

We took the train from King's Cross, changing a few times along the way to Hull in East Yorkshire. It used to be quite a fishing port when John was a boy, but a lot of that had ceased to exist. After London, it was such a let down. I found it to be very dirty and depressing. No wonder John left to find work in London. This was where he was born, so I kept my comments to myself for once in my life.

We stayed with his sister, the one whose wedding he took Barbara to and then asked her to marry him. No wonder I felt strange being there.

"Why are you acting different? You knew we were staying here."

"I know but being here where you proposed to another woman is a big deal to me."

"I didn't marry her though. I didn't really even ask her. She just thought I did, that's all."

"You didn't correct her even when she told her parents. You had her come to Fortescue House to tell her you couldn't marry her. I know. I was there watching the whole thing."

"Let's drop this, OK?"

He didn't want to be reminded about what a terrible person he was to Barbara. John wasn't good with confrontation.

"Right."

Subject dropped.

Jenny and Trevor (John's sister and her husband) owned a house in Hull, and we stopped to be with them for a bit. They lived in a row house—like you see in *Coronation Street*. It was a very depressing street—long, wet and dark looking. The toilet was outside, would you believe? They didn't have a fridge either. This was quite common at that time as most of the women shopped for food every day and bought just what they needed for that day. I had been spoilt at Miriam's using her fridge for so long.

We saw a lot of his dad and Vie (his stepmother) and a bit of his other sister and her husband. Auntie Nell (John's mom's sister) was well-liked and visited often. It was a whirlwind of people I met, and I liked most of them. It didn't really matter as I would see very little of any of them anyway.

One weekday, John said he was going out for a bit and would be back later. He'd left before I even realized he was gone. As it was a work day, both Jenny and Trevor were at work, and I didn't have a front door key. I sat all day long by myself waiting for someone to come home. Finally, near dinner time, Jenny returned from work.

"Where's John?" she asked me.

"I have no idea. He left this morning, and I haven't heard a word since. I've been sitting here all day by myself. I did call a friend of mine, and now that you're home, I'm going to meet him. You can tell your brother he can go screw himself."

And with that, I left.

My friend was Pete from Fortescue House, John's roommate. I had found out he went back home to Hull, so I called him mid-afternoon when I hadn't heard from John, to meet me in a town pub he picked. So, I met him there. Same guy with his red face, looking like he just farted. He stood up to greet me and knocked over some ashtray onto the floor. Some things never change. He got me a drink, and we were talking about old times in London when John came in.

"Hi, Pete," he said.

He didn't let Pete answer but grabbed my hand and out we went. Poor Pete.

"Where have you been all day long? I've been by myself at Jenny's and had to wait until she got home to go out with Pete." I was mad.

"I was with Stu." Stewart was a lifelong friend of John's. "We were drinking and talking, and I didn't think you'd like to come with me."

"Oh, go fuck yourself, you asshole."

I meant business when I swore, and he knew it. He had left all day and wasn't even apologizing to me for treating me like that. I just walked away. I was thinking, *am I making a big mistake? Is this how I'm going to be treated my whole life if I marry this clown? How will he get out of this one?*

I think I shocked the hell out of him. Not only was I not waiting for him at Jenny's, I was out drinking with a male friend. English women didn't act this way. They put up with all the crap their men threw at them. Well, not this woman!

Where was I going to go? Not back to Jenny's, that's for sure. I just started to run. I was scared and didn't know what to do for the best. I never thought about going back to the pub to say goodbye to Pete.

John finally caught up with me.

"I'm so sorry. I didn't realize you'd react like this just because I saw my old friend."

"You didn't tell me you were going for a drink with Stu, you just left, and I was alone in a strange house with no key to go anywhere. I thought you'd only be gone a while, not all day long. I called Pete and met him here. I don't need your permission to go out either. That's what you don't like. I wasn't just waiting for you at Jenny's. Screw you! I've told you before, you can't treat me like this and do whatever you want. We're supposed to be getting married. If you wanted someone to do what they are told, you should've married Barbara, not me."

"OK. OK. Stop yelling. People are looking at you. Let's go over there where it's a bit quieter and talk. Why are you getting so upset with me? I haven't done anything wrong really."

We went down the street where it was empty and not full of people coming out of the pubs.

"First of all, I didn't know where you were or how long you were going to be. I don't like being left alone in a strange house with no key. You could've told me you were going out with

Stu and how long you'd be gone for. That's just plain courtesy toward me. You just left. I can't live the rest of my life with you doing exactly what you want without any regard toward my feelings."

"I'm sorry. I just didn't think. I'm used to doing my own thing, I suppose."

"Garbage. You've been living with me for months. It's something about your hometown, I think. Let's go back to Jenny's. It's getting quite cold out."

So, we took the bus back to Jenny's house.

"You alright?" she asked John.

"Fine," we both answered.

I told John I was going upstairs to go to bed, and he could sleep elsewhere for the night. I was right back to where I was in London with this guy doing whatever he wanted. Seemed to me I'd have to give way and be more flexible when it came to him. Either that, or forget the whole thing. I didn't want to do that, so I talked myself round to seeing things more his way. But there was a limit to what I would or could take from him. *Why should I have to?*

We already had the discussion about screwing around, on his part, I wouldn't stand for it in any shape or form whatsoever. He knew a bit about my mom and dad and how he cheated on my mom, so he knew my thoughts. God, if you can't even be faithful to the person you marry, why marry? Screwing around for me was a non-starter. No way would I put up with it under any circumstances. John knew this very well. I told him I would be able to tell if he did fool around on me just by looking at him. That would also mean an instant divorce as well—no discussion. I mean, it wasn't as though I wasn't straightforward with this man.

So, the next day, all the drama was over. We would spend a few more days at Jenny's before going up to Scotland to visit even more relatives. I'd always wanted to see Scotland and should have a great advantage seeing it with someone who knew it quite well. John's dad was born in Cowdenbeath, just outside of Edinburgh, and had spent a lot of his childhood there.

A funny thing happened every night after supper. Trevor took off.

"Where does your husband go every night?" I asked Jenny when John wasn't around.

"To the pub," came the answer

"Why don't you go too?"

"That's just the way it is."

She was resigned to this fact. "Doesn't have to be, does it? What happens when you have kids? Can he just do whatever he wants?"

"That's just about it. It's always been this way. I'm used to it now that we're married."

Trevor first came home from work to be fed. He just sat down and was waited on hand and foot by his wife who also had worked all day long. But after her work, she had to go grocery shopping, then prepare their dinner. Trev only had to wolf down his dinner, have a nice bath and leave for the pub, returning after closing time. Nice gig if you can get it, eh?

"What a horrible future life for you."

But I could see that's the way it was, and she was putting up with it. I thought it was insane, but I wasn't married to him, was I? John didn't look so bad now. It wasn't just that Trev left her by herself all night every night, he also spent a lot of money on beer, coming home plastered most nights. They were trying to buy this house for God's sake. His money was his—full stop. He gave her housekeeping money to buy food with, but if she needed anything else, it came from her money. What a setup. What would happen once the kids came? Not my problem, but the whole thing made me sick.

I guess I was too out of it to realize I was in the same boat, so to speak. Didn't John just leave me alone for a whole day to go drinking with one of his buddies without so much as a phone call to say where he was or what he was up to? The difference in my mind was that I did something about it. I went out with another guy to show how much I wouldn't be treated like I didn't matter. Jenny just accepted that this was how her life was going to be. How sad.

It was time to leave for Scotland. I sure wasn't sorry to say goodbye to Jenny and Trev. She was in for one hell of a life, but that was none of my business. I did like John's dad and Vie though and hoped they would come over to my world. Margaret and Geoff I only saw a few times, so I had no opinion of them at all.

The plan was to take a bus to Newcastle and then the train to Edinburgh. We got off the bus in Newcastle, and John told me to ask the bus conductor where the train station was. I did. Was this man really speaking in English? I didn't understand a word the man said and could see John laughing his head off at me. He had to get the directions, and I could see he had to pay attention to what the man said. Dirty trick. They called people who came from Newcastle Geordies. I don't know why. Even the rest of England couldn't understand these guys, so I didn't feel so bad.

So, we got the train to Edinburgh. We hadn't pre-booked a place to stay for the few days we were going to be there. So, we trudged around and found a bed and breakfast to stay in.

Edinburgh is a great city. I loved it immediately, not like I loved London, of course, but pretty close. The castle arising above the town was something to see. We had the time to visit some attractions in Edinburgh, and we did just that. We, of course, went to visit Edinburgh Castle. We just walked around looking at what there was to see. I can't even remember if there were proper tours then, I suppose there were, but we didn't fork out the pounds to take one. Why break our cheap habit of thinking we knew what everything was. How ridiculous we were, but that's what happened (or didn't, so to speak). It was quite the place, and I enjoyed every moment. What a view from the castle. Turns out, John's dad used to be a guard there. Isn't that cool?

The main street is called Princes St., but I have always called it Princess St. as in Princess Diana, not the plural of prince. I suppose someone called it Princess at one point, and it just stuck with me. It wasn't until I was reading a Bill Bryson book that I noted the spelling, and I knew he couldn't be wrong. Anyway, it's a lovely street with a floral clock growing in the gardens. In its heart stands Scott Monument. It's dedicated to the poet Sir Walter Scott. There are 287 steps to the top of this spire, and it's 200 feet high. Its steps are made of stone and are very windy, steep and narrow, and I found it very difficult to climb them. I am very afraid of heights, so reaching the top wasn't a joy for me. The views over Edinburgh were/are spectacular, and I suppose worth being afraid over. We did get a certificate saying we had done the climb. I wish I still had it as I doubt I would ever climb those stairs again.

Another attraction that I liked was the Portuguese Cannon. This was a cannon sitting on top of a steep hill called Calton Hill. I remember straddling the cannon while having my picture taken. What a tourist!

Even though we stayed in Edinburgh, his family lived in Cowdenbeath, a short train ride away. Cowdenbeath was a very quaint little town or maybe even a village. I don't know. There used to be a lot of coal mining done there, and some of John's relatives used to be miners. I met some cousins and their spouses as well as his Uncle Dave and Aunt Janet (John's dad's brother and his wife). Their place was immaculate. Not a hair was out of place. It was a joy for me to see after living in all those messy, dirty places in London.

Although these two were speaking in English, I couldn't understand a word being said. Cowdenbeath is in

Fifeshire, Scotland, and the accent is brutal and completely uncomprehensable. So, when they laughed, I laughed. When asked a direct question, I looked to John to answer. I think after a bit they came to realize I didn't understand them. Aunt Janet cooked us mince and tatties. This is mince beef served over mashed potatoes and quite Scottish. It was heaven to me. The best cooking I'd had in quite a long time. She sure went to the top of my list of favourite relatives in this place. They were both very nice people, and we got along smashingly. This was where John's dad was born.

We went from this dream house of cleanliness and fine cooking to a dump. It was up the hill and around the corner. It was where John's mom's sister and family lived. What a pig pen it was. Or maybe I just remember it so because Janet's place was so homey and clean. We were offered some biscuits and tea as we, of course, had just eaten a rather large meal. I tried to be polite and listen to the conversation, without success. John's cousin Andy was there, and they seemed to get along very well, so I left them to it. I couldn't wait to get out of that place, but could be civil while John did his thing. I was secretly hoping I'd never have to come back here again. To top it off, they had this rather large dog who particularly liked MY crotch to sniff. Nobody stopped him, so I hit him hard on his nose. Dogs are not my favourite. I love cats.

Man was it cool there, as in cold, considering it was September. I had my leather coat I bought at Petticoat Lane for £4 on, but it was still not warm. At least it didn't rain most of the time we were there. I had learnt a long time ago, any day without rain on this island was a good day.

Chapter Fourteen

I ENJOYED MY TIME IN Cowdenbeath and Edinburgh. Now I was ready to go home. We still had to go back down to London to catch our flight from Heathrow to Toronto. We were flying B.O.A.C. That meant British Overseas Airways Corporation. I've also heard it called "Boys Overseas After Crumpet" which was highly appropriate for this country.

So, we returned to London, staying at a bed and breakfast run by a man from Montreal. No discount for being Canadian either! We went to Lynn and Dennis' new flat to say goodbye to them. Nothing had changed there either. They both seemed quite happy in their situation. I still don't know how Lynn managed to stay in London past her time limit on her passport. I guess she had a job and wasn't a drain on British society, so they let her. She didn't seem to be envious of the fact I was going home. She apparently had joined Dennis in the pot smoking, so I wished her good luck with that. She had never been a true friend to me.

While we were there, John tried out Dennis' new bike. He asked me to get on the back too, but I wasn't interested in riding with anyone who thought the gas was on the left, not right like I was used to. I had taken motorcycle lessons when I was a teenager. I loved bikes. Especially then when helmets were nonexistent. So, I missed the bike ride, only of course to find out that in Britain, the gas is on the right like everywhere else. Glad I didn't give a reason to John for my not joining him on the bike. Did I ever feel stupid.

So, we said bye to them. Can't remember if I gave her my address or not. Probably not. She paid me no attention when we lived in the same city, so I doubted she'd bother to write me in Canada nor I to her. I didn't like Dennis very much. I thought he was a little weasel the way he treated her all these months. But I no longer had to see either of them again if I didn't want to. *We'll see how it goes,* I thought.

We also found out where Tacus had gone. He lived around Bayswater area now. I couldn't believe the state of him. He opened the door to us, and we all stood on the doorstep to talk. He looked awful—very thin and gaunt looking. Smoking a bit of pot hadn't done this to him. I didn't really want to know as I was going home and couldn't help him at all. I really liked him. He had once taken me out when we lived at Fortescue House. We had seen *Romeo and Juliet* the movie together, more for company on my part than an actual date. Don't really know how he felt about me, but I found him too intense for him to be anything but my friend. So, we said goodbye.

I had already said goodbye to Jackie and her family. I went over one Saturday before we went up to Scotland and saw her, her mom and dad, and even her brother who I had rarely seen. Then we were off to the pub to say bye to some people there. While at the pub, Jackie confessed to me she'd slept with John (Aussie from Fortescue House).

"How could you? He's a creep, Jackie!"

"He had this way of looking at me that made me feel good about myself."

What could I say? Once again, none of my business who she slept with. But it did give me some insight into why she kept sleeping with different men. I suppose it made her feel wanted for at least a little while.

John didn't want to come to see Jackie. I think he thought she was a "bit of a one" as well, and certainly, he wouldn't put himself out to say goodbye to her. I would miss Jackie. She'd been a very good friend to me even though I didn't agree with her lifestyle nor her mine. We agreed to write, and I sincerely hoped she would. I had her address and gave her my mom's.

I would sincerely miss living in London. I got to live in a magnificent city for a short time, make some great friends, work in two different places with lots of interesting people, see unforgettable sights, have a baby sham or two in some fantastic pubs, have sex, live with a man, and get engaged to be married. I also learned I could look after myself in every sense of the word because I had to.

Isn't that why we travel—to see differences? If everything were the same, what would be the point? I was quite sure I would return many times to this lovely city, maybe someday with my own kids in tow.

So, here I was back on a plane again. This time, I was going home with someone I wasn't quite sure about. But I was extremely grateful, lucky and very happy not to be going home pregnant.

By the way, my name is Lynn.

THE END (FOR NOW)